PRAISE FOR
MEASURING UP

"We finally have an exciting book that logically blends together neuroscience and humanism. Dr. Linzey's book, *Measuring Up*, is based on the latest scientific research of neuroplasticity, coaches your children to becoming smarter and happier students while enhancing their cognitive skill fundamentals and putting the "fun and ease" back into learning. It's gratifying to know that it is never too late for anyone to become smarter, think faster, improve their memory and realize more potential."

MARCUS A. ERLING, M.D.
LAS VEGAS, NV

"For the millions of parents out there who want the best opportunity to succeed for their children, this *is* the way. Dr. Linzey's book explains in plain terms the complexity of neuroplasticity and how every child has the potential to benefit from it. *Measuring Up* is an impressively well-thought-out program embedding everything from the concept of an open mindset learning to dynamic brain training and coaching uniquely catered to each child. Powerfully written and extraordinarily informative for all."

SANDRA FONTENLA
MEDICAL PHYSICIST
MANHATTAN, NY

"As an optometrist, I encounter patients from three to ninety-nine years old who I cannot help with glasses alone. In many cases it is not a visual condition causing poor school or work performance but a visual processing or cognitive skills problem. These individuals need to have their mental acuity improved.

Knowing Dr. Linzey for over twenty years, I have seen her change the lives of hundreds of her students and patients. Through her techniques, individuals of all ages can improve their brains ability to utilize the information their eyes are importing to the visual cortex. With the proper tools, everyone can condition their brain to work efficiently and obtain the peak performance."

LISA BENHAM, O.D.

YORBA LINDA, CA

"*Measuring Up*, by Tere Linzey, is a must-read for parents and educators. It provides very helpful information and practical tools to help your child as well as students in the classroom."

RIM HINCKLEY

HEAD OF SCHOOL

THE GENEVA SCHOOL OF MANHATTAN

MANHATTAN, NY

MEASURING UP

the go-to guide for
parents and students
looking for an edge
in the hyper-competitive
world of education

DR. TERE LINZEY

FASTBREAK Press
Paperback ISBN: 978-0-9962630-0-9
E-book ISBN: 978-0-9862474-8-4

This book is dedicated to all those individuals who coached me, taught me to be coachable, and pointed me in the right direction when I fell off of the straight and narrow. It is also dedicated to all those who taught me that what we think and do repeatedly will inevitably create our destiny.

ACKNOWLEDGMENTS

Many thanks to people from my youth, like Karen Edgar Knight, Dr. L. L. Merrifield, Marguerite Curl, Evelyn Hobbs, and Dr. Larry Robinson—just a few of the standout educators, coaches, and advisors who have shared their invaluable wisdom and experience with me. I would also like to thank all my current and former students. It has been my great honor to teach you, coach you, and learn from you.

I would like to thank my parents for their love and support and for allowing me to grow up in a community where I could learn, through the game of basketball, how to play the game of life.

Many thanks also go out to dear friends Dr. Lisa Behnam, Dr. Susan Villa, Erin Murphy, Marnie Woehr, Nita Pettigrew, Heather Crane, and Sandi Pierce—the kind of friends whose very presence lets you know you are becoming the person you want to be. Their words of encouragement have resonated so strongly in my head, for so long, that I can barely hear my fearful doubts anymore. The good luck of finding even one friend of their caliber would have been extraordinary, but to find seven of them is a damn miracle!

I sincerely extend my gratitude to Iris Dart, for her friendship and help in pushing this project forward, and to my editor, Ruby Peru, for her expertise, patience, and steadfast guidance.

Lastly, a sincere thank you to those scientists, educators, authors, doctors, researchers, and other specialists who have helped to educate me and who have made it possible for me to apply my knowledge in the service of others.

Thank you to Jeffrey Munks for revisions.

CONTENTS

FOREWORD

MEASURING UP

At the conclusion of an address to a group of parents and alumni some years ago, a Cate School senior was asked what her most valuable takeaway from her high school experience would be. This was an extraordinarily high-achieving student, a talented athlete, and a community leader. She would matriculate at Harvard in the fall. Her answer: "I know who I am."

Identity—that critical understanding that compels us all throughout our lives and that is particularly acute in adolescence—is the Holy Grail for any student who would presume to make something of him or her self; to "measure up," if you will. Central to that journey is an understanding of the characteristics, aptitudes, interests, and challenges that combine to make us who we are. For all students, even the precocious young woman headed off to Harvard, that is a complex, often vexing, and all-consuming effort—wonderful at its terminus (assuming there is one), but neither easy nor predictable along the way.

What students need, especially in relation to their capacity to learn and grow, are tools, practices, and inroads to their own unique character of cognition. Despite appearances, no one has it all figured out. Like adults, young people look around to see if others are struggling with concepts or expectations. They make judgments—most of which are flawed and uninformed—because they are intensely aware of their own difficulties, yet can find no evidence of the same in others. They worry that they will under-perform, disappoint parents or friends or teammates, become less than who they want to be.

This is a cycle we see all too often in schools, even among those we would identify as high-achieving, high-aspiring students. The parents of these talented young people are often heavily in-vested in potential outcomes and are trying whenever possible to be helpful. In most cases, despite the best of intentions all around, the "help" is less productive or efficacious than it might be, often causing conflict, heartache, and even further erosion of confidence on the part of student and parents.

The simple truth, of course, which Dr. Linzey explains so clearly in the pages that follow, is that we can learn to be our best. In fact, we are built to do just that. Our brains are wired for change and progress—not in some rote or static fashion, but organically and through evolving patterns that produce under-standing. What's more, the answer lies not in what someone—a parent or a tutor or even a teacher—might do for a student, but rather in what a student might learn to do for him or herself.

We have enough young people who are driven to achieve-ment by forces outside themselves, but one wonders if such people can lay claim to the very sense of self so crucial not sim-ply to scholastic success but to goal-setting, life-building, even happiness.

Here, it seems, is where Dr. Linzey's work holds particular promise. If we can in fact gain access to the manner in which we each learn and use that knowledge to hone the skills and habits that contribute to learning, how many obstacles and impedi-ments have we summarily removed from our paths? Thankfully, this is not an "if" question anymore, for the means to journey down that road exist within this text.

Having worked personally with Dr. Linzey and seen the byproducts of her efforts with students at Cate School, I con-fess that I can't understand why anyone—parent, teacher, or student—wouldn't seek out her methods. They are powerful, personal, and immensely impactful. As Dr. Linzey points out, "There is no rushing genius." But certainly there is genius in all of us. Best not wait to begin the search for it.

Benjamin Williams IV
Headmaster, Cate School
August 7, 2014

MEASURING UP

CHAPTER 1

BASKETBALL AND BRAIN SCIENCE

My Journey from Head *Coach to* Head *Coach*

Life can only be understood backwards—
but it must be lived forwards.

SØREN KIERKEGAARD

I can still remember walking out of the 2009 "Learning and the Brain" conference at Harvard, my mind abuzz with the latest research on learning and achievement, feeling that I had finally found the one subject area that pulled all my interests together: neuroscience. Yet I wasn't a scientist, nor did I aspire to become one. My resume declared me to be a doctor of educational psychology and a teacher of physical education and special education with master's degrees in marriage and family therapy, education administration, and school psychology. Plus I harbored a passion for playing and coaching women's basketball. Calling my interests diverse would be an understatement.

My anchor subject, the thing that formed the basis of how I thought, actually seems the most out of place: basketball. During undergraduate school, I played for Phillips University in Oklahoma, on a national championship team. Then I enjoyed the good fortune of studying the game of basketball with famed Indiana Hoosiers coach Bobby Knight, and his wife, Karen Vieth Edgar, one of the best women's basketball coaches in Oklahoma. For thirteen years afterward, I coached women's basketball through-out Oklahoma, receiving the distinction of Oklahoma Coach of the Year before taking over as coach at California's Beverly Hills High School. Thanks to the excellent training I received from my mentors, I turned each school's losing streak into a championship season.

As coach, I designed drills for offense, defense, footwork, free-throws, and every other aspect of the game, customizing the drills to remediate each individual player's shortcomings. Later, when I taught high school, whether I found myself in the field of physical education, English, or special education, I used the same approach: drilling fundamentals.

In sports, fundamentals are the primary building blocks of any athlete's development. That's why, each time I took on a new women's basketball team, I found that while certain players may excel at specialties such as jump shots or free throws, if the en-tire team didn't possess the full range of fundamental skills, it simply would not win. So when I began to work as an academic teacher, I was surprised to find that my fellow teachers did not always utilize this approach in education. In fact, I'll wager if you surveyed any random group of school teachers and asked them, "What are the fundamental building blocks of learning?", they couldn't answer the question. That's because this is a question not for teachers, but for neuroscientists.

Neuroscientists are the people who discover and codify how the brain works and how people learn best. While their discov-eries should be required reading for any educator, for a variety of reasons, neuroscientific advances haven't yet found their way into mainstream education. That might just be because the rev-elations made by neuroscientists in the past twenty years are so immense that, if properly applied, they would bring about a complete overhaul of the American educational system as we know it. The most recent, groundbreaking, neuroscientific ad-vances have in fact revealed an even more specific sub-specialty:

neuroplasticity, which is the science of how the brain changes based upon its experiences.

The study of neuroplasticity has yielded breakthrough findings that changed the course of my personal and professional life and it's what drove me to write this book. The findings? *We now know that the brain can actually teach itself to be smarter, faster, more creative, and more logical!*

Maybe because of the high expectations of my grandmother, who was voted an Oklahoma "Teacher of the Year" several times, I have always been headstrong—one who does what it takes to learn and grow and change for the better in my life. But, as a teacher, I have come across many students, and even parents, who find it difficult to take the necessary steps to change. They want to grow, they want to advance, but the path toward success seems too arduous. I have also seen many underperforming students strive for better grades by hiring tutors, joining study groups, and taking test-prep classes, but they somehow still don't reach their goals.

In addition, I have met quite a few high-achieving students who simply aren't satisfied with doing what comes naturally. They want to achieve more, faster, and more efficiently. I sympathize. I love efficiency, and I love change. I love knowing I have the power to move my life in any direction I want, and I hate to think there are people who want to change and grow and learn, yet face hurdles they don't know how to overcome. This is why I felt such a sense of revelation that day in Harvard Yard, when I stepped out of the "Learning and the Brain" conference and into the February snow. I had just been introduced to the science of neuroplasticity, the missing key that held the answers for how I could help students jump those hurdles.

Buttoning my coat against Massachusetts's February chill, I knew I had to link my career as an educator and educational psychologist to neuroscience's revelatory scientific breakthroughs. That meant bringing the findings of neuroplasticity out of the science lab and into the schools and homes of ordinary people. People who, like me, value intelligence. People who, like me, can think of little they would like to achieve more than being smarter and happier people, with smarter and happier families, through the "magic" of neuroplasticity.

DISCOVERING EDUCATIONAL PSYCHOLOGY

It's funny to think about now, but I got my bachelor's degree in physical education, a subject about as far from neuroplasticity as it is possible to be. Back then basketball was my life, but you need to understand where I'm from: Oklahoma. There, women's basketball is second only to football as a state-wide obsession.

After college I worked as a high school physical education teacher while earning my master's degree in education administration, but when I finished I realized I didn't want to become a school principal. I had certainly learned a lot about how schools work, and I had enjoyed that field of study, but by this point I knew I could never become the desk-bound, administrative type. Instead, I applied for my first coaching job at a highly-ranked 5A Oklahoma high school.

Honestly, I only did it for interview practice. I certainly didn't expect to be selected from a pool of 167 applicants, but I was. The superintendent told me if he hired me I'd be the youngest 5A coach in the state. Cocky as ever, I shot back, "Aren't you the youngest 5A superintendent in the state? Maybe Oklahoma needs a change." He liked my attitude, and so it began.

I spent four years at that school and turned the program around 180 degrees. My girls became state champions, and I moved on to coach teams at one school after another, gaining a little bit of renown in the tiny, but intensely competitive, world of Oklahoma women's high school sports. Next, the principal from Beverly Hills High School, where the girls hadn't won a game in (dear God!) five years, made me an offer. I couldn't resist the challenge, or the weather, so I moved on and turned their program around until the team went all the way to the CIF (California Interscholastic Federation) quarter finals.

Though most Beverly Hills High students were accustomed to a life of wealth and privilege, my players learned very quickly that I didn't know what the word entitlement meant. I taught each player how to work hard on mastering the fundamentals of our sport. Then, when my girls started winning their games, they finally got it. Hard work and fundamentals pay off—in wins, in pride, in self-confidence.

After four years, I had accomplished what I intended to do there, and I needed a new challenge. Much to the consternation of my players, friends, family, and colleagues, I decided to change careers. No one understood, of course. Everyone in Beverly Hills simply knew me as "Coach," but I knew I held more potential. Just as my players had grown and changed over the course of the past few years, so had I, and I had actually outgrown coaching basketball.

I had always enjoyed changing how my players looked at the game of basketball. I enjoyed figuring out how best to get inside the girls' heads and how to coach each individual player so that she would improve, stay positive, stay focused, and, most of all, want that win more than anything else in the world. If a player lacked a fundamental skill, I became obsessed with finding what blocked her, remediating that, and putting things right. Basically, what I liked best about coaching was the psychology of it all. So, after Beverly Hills High School's 1996 basketball season, I returned to college, simultaneously working for my special education teaching certification and driving an hour and a half away for classes toward a master's degree in school psychology.

Soon I took on work as a special education teacher, where I came to the realization that teaching is just coaching in a smaller room. I made a point of teaching my students that the power to succeed lay inside of them as long as they stayed focused, believed in themselves, and worked their fundamental skills day in and day out. No matter their IQs, no matter their test scores, I believed my students could improve themselves as long as, like ballplayers, they remained focused on fundamentals. With this attitude I did see improvement in my students, but not as much as I expected. After looking at the bigger picture I realized that parental and family support, or lack of it, made a much bigger difference in my students' lives than I ever would.

I wanted to help my students' families better support and encourage them, so, even though I was still pursuing my doctorate, I added an additional set of courses on marriage and family therapy to my course load. In studying this fascinating aspect of psychology, I observed that traditional therapeutic techniques didn't always work. So, as part of my psychology doctorate program, I also looked into alternative therapies, such as hypnotherapy and neuro-linguistic programming, and wrote my PhD dissertation on the vast field of alternatives to traditional psychology. But even with my PhD in hand I wasn't satisfied. I went to conference after conference, looking for that missing key I could use to help struggling students, and their parents, shift how they perceived the educational process, make a change for the better, and see results quickly. I wanted to get to the core of learning and answer the question, "How can people improve themselves rapidly, in a lasting way?"

Finally, when I attended the 2009 "Learning and the Brain" conference at Harvard, I realized the answer to this great mystery lay inside the science of neuroplasticity. From there it took one more year to receive my certification in neuropsychology assessment from University of California, Berkeley. Finally I felt I knew not just how people learn, *but how their brains learn how to learn*. I realized that was what I ultimately wanted to teach. I wanted to empower students to take charge of their own learning processes. Back when I used to study coaching with Bobby Knight, he always said, "You have to be a 'student of the game' of basketball." Well, I had taken that advice to the highest level I could by becoming a student of the game of being a student.

After all of those courses and degrees, I packed up my potential and headed out to change a few things. That's how I became the director of counseling and education psychologist at Cate

School, a prestigious co-educational boarding school on the California coast. In my two years there, I utilized the principals of neuroplasticity; my knowledge of cognitive skills, processing, executive function, and social and emotional wellness; and my own long-held belief in the importance of fundamentals, to develop a one-on-one cognitive skills training program I now call BrainMatterZ , which is designed to help ambitious students achieve their own personal versions of excellence. Much to my delight, Cate School also let me coach a little basketball!

THE WORLD'S BEST BRAINS

Not just as an educator, but as a citizen of the planet, I'm concerned with solving life's greatest riddles. How can we end war and promote peace in the nations of the world? How can human beings reduce pollution while improving technology? Is it possible to bring about an end to disease and famine? What's the most efficient way to help victims of natural disasters? What great new heights can be achieved in the arts and human expression? Each successive generation attempts to answer great questions such as these, and, as a result, we have seen true genius appear on the world stage—from Beethoven to Benjamin Franklin to Einstein to Steve Jobs, the list is endless. But we have also seen immense gains in art, science, and technology be overshadowed by poor decision making, loss of momentum, prejudice, and lack of foresight.

Educators aspire to teach students who will wonder why things like war and disease still haven't been eradicated, then go forth and eradicate them. Ambitious students, hungry for knowledge, dream of becoming those great inventors, politicians, artists, and activists who will change the world for the better. Yet when problems persist over millennia, repeatedly confounding even the world's greatest minds, each successive generation wonders why this must be so. Enter neuroplasticity. Perhaps, just perhaps, says this new way of looking at the human brain, we now possess the long-sought ability to teach ourselves to be smarter, wiser people.

Perhaps now is the time to tackle the world's greatest problems ... with the world's best brains.

Great problems have always been solved by those with ambition—high achievers, if you will. Though high achievers show their intelligence, confidence, and ambition in different ways, they often display a spark quite early in life, prompting parents and teachers to wonder if these children will be the leaders of tomorrow. Such students tend to be big-picture thinkers who are able to see the full length and breadth of any playing field (be it physical or academic) and instinctively aspire to conquer it. In sports, they push to win. In school, they strive to develop their own unique critical-thinking skills, while also earning high grades. Even in conversation these charismatic students challenge preconceived notions and promote new ideas. Such high achievers are often marked by a strong moral compass and frequently spend their energy working to improve relationships and defend the innocent or weak. Naturally self-confident, these children, marked by a sense of right and wrong and a desire to make the world a better place, are sometimes called visionaries.

Many theories exist as to how people turn out to be high achievers and visionaries, but no one cause is certain. We only know that when we see a child who naturally breaks large goals into smaller goals, achieves those goals independently, and recognizes each achievement with confidence, we have found someone special. When children can take risks, believe in their chances of succeeding, and build upon their successes with additional ambition, teachers and parents know these bright children should be given every opportunity to succeed. Such students tend to be grounded, sometimes very quiet, but willing and eager to stretch beyond their comfort zones, try new things, and persist without giving up. These children have the natural creativity to create new pathways to success in any endeavor until that success is achieved. Somehow they instinctively understand that each new failure brings them closer to eventual success.

Please know I'm not talking about some new race of superbeing. These children are all around us, in every school and classroom in America, and across the socioeconomic spectrum, but they are still children, and as such they remain vulnerable and in need of guidance. Those leadership traits, that natural kindness, that inherent ambition and instinctive resilience, must be nurtured to ensure these children build upon their skills and become brighter every day. No matter how brilliant the child may be, parents are crucial to that process.

For any child, having a parent actively involved in his or her schooling is the best determinate of success. This is no less true for driven, high-achieving students than for those with academic difficulties. When parents encourage learning and achievement with praise, stimulating environments, and intelligent conversation, this brings out confidence and ambition in children. Yet, even when they come from highly enriching backgrounds, students sometimes still fail to achieve their best for reasons neither they, nor their parents, fully understand.

Public and private schools that tend to attract bright high-achievers develop a culture all their own, and while this culture supports scholastic pursuits, it also tends to foster competition and social pressure, which can lead to bright children internalizing their anxieties, even to the point of developing eating disorders and depression. Test anxiety can also plague even the smartest students, who find it incredibly frustrating to be unable to demonstrate their knowledge when it really counts. In such cases, educators know there is a problem but often don't understand its root cause.

Many parents, communities, and schools operate on the principle that low-achieving children need the most help, while high-achievers will manage on their own, even though evidence shows this simply isn't true.[1] High achievers often hide academic or personal shortcomings behind their amazing verbal skills. They compensate for poor reading with excellent memorization, cover up anxiety and depression with scholastic achievements. Wherever there is great potential for success, there also lurk the same social, emotional, cognitive, and academic problems that all other children experience. However, how to help bright children be happy and perform up to their best abilities is a topic in hot dispute in today's competitive academic environments.

Parents often go to great expense to help their children get ahead—enrolling them in tutoring, after-school activities, and test-prep courses—only to find their children, academically, right back where they started, minus hundreds, perhaps thousands, of dollars spent on supplemental education. Of course, certain academic gains can be achieved with traditional tutoring, but these gains tend to be superficial and short-lived. In fact, if an ambitious child suffers from a learning deficit of any kind, such accelerated education can actually compound the child's anxiety and frustration around learning. Luckily, the latest findings in neuroplasticity finally explain why working harder doesn't necessarily make a student smarter.[2]

The fact is that neither memorizing lists of state capitals nor drilling science facts provides students with the type of advancement they need to make their learning experiences more enjoyable and efficient. Neuroplasticity researchers teach us that these programs address only academic achievement, not the root of learning. These ambitious students don't need tutors, but brain trainers.[3] Just as basketball players need coaches who can drill them in the fundamentals of the game until they can coordinate all those skills for a win, academic students also need training to understand and practice the fundamentals of learning.

The highly involved parents of these ambitious children sometimes find themselves derisively labeled "Helicopter Parents" or "Tiger Moms" or "Hothouse Parents" and stand accused of micromanaging their children's lives. It's no wonder many parents feel they can't win; inevitably society sends them the message they are either too involved or not involved enough. But there is no denying the fact that children need guidance to get the most out of any educational system. In addition, they need the support, encouragement, and sometimes "tough love" that a highly involved parent provides. In fact, this type of parental involvement actually helps them build the neural pathways that lead to high achievement and a love of learning.[4]

But a mother need not constantly arm herself with flash cards, and a father need not turn every dinner table conversation into a teachable moment. New research has revealed that the trick to best-practice parenting resides not in drilling children with information, but in helping them increase their innate ability to identify, process, analyze, and draw conclusions about the information they already take in on a day-to-day basis. In fact, we now know that in order to truly promote lifelong learning, parents, tutors, and enrichment programs should focus less on teaching facts and figures and more on improving something called "cognitive skills."[5]

CHAPTER 2

COGNITIVE SKILLS

The Fundamentals of Learning

It starts with the complete command of fundamentals.

JESSE OWENS

ognitive skills are the fundamental skills we need in order to learn. Just as athletes must develop the fundamental skills of any game, so, too, students must master the fundamentals of learning. Cognitive skills are evident in our ability to quickly understand, analyze, and remember the things we hear, see, and experience. For instance, algebra is not a cognitive skill, nor is English literature. However, sustained attention, long-term memory, and logic are. Cognitive skills enable us to learn academic subjects the way fertile earth, sunshine, and water enable plants to grow. With that in mind, it makes more sense to provide a tulip with earth, sun, and water to enable its maturation than to hold up a picture of a beautiful bloom and tell the tulip bulb, "Make yourself look like this! Memorize it! Quickly!"

Following is a list of the cognitive skills students use when they learn. In fact, we all use these cognitive skills, all day long, for everything from finding a parking space, to recalling the words to a favorite song, to making complex vacation plans, to, of course, taking academic tests. Be forewarned: the following list will reveal nothing you can learn in a traditional way, such as drilling, memorizing, or quizzing.

Cognitive Skills List

- **Attention Skills:** The ability to attend to incoming information.
  - o **Sustained Attention:** The ability to focus on a task long enough to complete it.
  - o **Selective Attention:** The ability to focus on a task despite sensory distractions such as noise, touching, and visual input.
- **Divided Attention:** Also known as multi-tasking;" the ability to remember information from task A while performing unrelated mental operations from task B.
- **Memory:** The ability to store and recall information.
  - o **Long-term Memory:** The ability to recall information stored in the past—useful for spelling, mathematics, and reading comprehension where understanding new facts utilizes a base of prior knowledge.
  - o **Short-term/Working Memory:** Another aspect of multi-tasking, this is the ability to hold information in mind while performing a different mental task; for instance, remembering a list of instructions while executing them.
- **Logic:** The ability to form concepts, solve problems, and execute reasoning skills using novel information or procedures.
- **Deductive Reasoning:** The ability to draw conclusions and create solutions by analyzing relationships.
- **Processing Speed:** The ability to perform the above cognitive tasks with alacrity, despite distractions.
  - o **Auditory Processing:** The ability to analyze, blend, and segment sounds.
  - o **Visual Processing:** The ability to perceive, analyze, and think in visual images.
- **Executive Function:** The ability to manage the collection of cognitive, emotional, and behavioral functions, particularly during active, novel, problem solving events. Executive functioning is so named because it concerns the part of the brain that could be considered "upper management." Executive function includes the following subcategories:

o **Inhibit:** The ability to resist temptation or to avoid acting on impulse.

o **Shift:** The ability to transition easily between one aspect of a task to another; flexibility.

o **Emotional Control:** The ability to control emotional responses and impulses.

o **Initiate:** The self-motivation that enables someone to get started on a new problem-solving task.

o **Working Memory:** The capacity to hold information in mind while performing a task, in order to carry out multi-step activities.

o **Plan/Organize:** The ability to sequence a series of steps in order to manage current and future-oriented tasks

o **Materials Organization:** The ability to maintain an orderly work space or storage space.

o **Monitor:** The ability to self-assess during or after completing a task, and the ability to evaluate the effect one's behavior has on others.

After glancing over the list, I'm sure you noticed none of the skills mentioned are the kind of things that normally show up in a tutor's review session or on the syllabus of an SAT prep class. Instead, cognitive skills are the brain functions that enable such learning to occur. Chances are, whether you are a parent or educator, you have no idea how to teach these skills. Used to administering spelling tests, quizzing students on historical facts, and checking answers to math problems, most parents and teachers are lost when faced with how to teach processing speed, sustained attention, or working memory. In the interest of helping students learn and grow more quickly and efficiently, I made it my business to figure out how to do just that. For the past six years, teaching the brain to learn how to learn has been my fascination and passion.

Regardless of their IQ or socioeconomic status, few students enter school with a fully developed, comprehensive set of cognitive skills. After all, every childhood is different. Some children will naturally develop the ability to process auditory information such as verbal instructions and songs, while others tend to favor visual processing, perhaps due to a childhood that emphasized picture books and reading. Meanwhile, children whose childhoods have not given them practice using executive function skills oftentimes compensate with amazing verbal abilities. A child from a large family may develop the ability to concentrate, despite distractions early in life, while an only child may come to first grade completely unpracticed in blocking out ambient noise. Every brain develops in a manner that is unique to its experiences.

Even the most stimulating, happy childhood will produce a child with unevenly developed cognitive skills, and there is nothing wrong with that. After all, our cognitive skills contribute greatly to our personalities, and we wouldn't all want to be alike. But where academics are concerned, we achieve best results when we work to build each and every one of our cognitive skills toward peak performance.

Bright children usually compensate for one underfunctioning cognitive skill by relying on another well-developed one. For instance, if a student has trouble with the visual memorizing required for copying off the blackboard, he can simply rely on his auditory memory to remember the information from the teacher's lectures. If another student has trouble sustaining attention in class, she can catch up on the information by reading the textbook later. Anyone who has ever been a student knows these little tricks are second nature for getting through school. But although these strategies have helped many a bright student enter the university of his or her choice, they actually require the student to work harder than necessary.

All that extra work spent on compensating for underperforming cognitive skills means less enjoyment of the learning process and more time the child needs to spend studying. Consequently, less time is available for simple childhood pleasures, which are also important to psychological, social, and academic development. But now, utilizing the latest advances in brain science, psychologists can assess any student's vast menu of cognitive skills, practice those which may be lacking, and help students improve, in order to learn everything more quickly, with less effort.

When students can read with better understanding, focus more intently despite distractions, and process information more rapidly, learning becomes more fun. Even more importantly, when students begin to understand their own learning processes the way today's brain scientists do, they gain a fascination with learning itself that ensures a lifelong love of learning, which has been shown to result in increased levels of overall happiness and more mental acuity right into old age. Sadly, today's schools and teachers—already overwhelmed by everything from behavior problems to bureaucracy—rarely have the opportunity to stay abreast of the latest advances in neuroplasticity. Hence, another important reason for writing this book: to guide parents in helping bright, driven children achieve their highest academic potential, greatest personal happiness, and most fulfilling contribution to society—all with ease and a sense of fun.

Cognitive skills are a subset of the fascinating subject of neuroplasticity: the science of how the brain grows and changes throughout life. "Neuro" relates to the nervous system, and "plasticity" relates to the brain's flexible and ever-evolving nature. If you have never heard of neuroplasticity before reading this book, don't panic. Even though its findings have changed everything in terms of our knowledge of how people learn, this is a very new field.

Based upon studies that have been underway since the 1980s, this science only emerged into public consciousness early in this century, when scientists stated publicly and unequivocally that the brain, which was previously thought to establish a set intelligence, or IQ level, quite early in life, is actually a constantly evolving organ with an almost infinite ability to learn, get smarter, and repair its own defects.[6] This means that whether you are a driven, high-performing child working to achieve your life's highest potential or a victim of brain damage attempting to regain lost functions, with proper assessment and practice you can improve your brain to a limitless degree.

Scientists and psychologists used to compare the brain to a computer, suggesting that it is programmed in infancy and destined to utilize that same programming throughout life; but we now understand that, just like the rest of your body, the brain never stops adapting and developing.[7] For instance, if you should become blind, your body gradually would adapt by improving your listening skills and using your fingers to read Braille. If you should become unable to walk, your body gradually would adapt to the use of a wheelchair by increasing your arm strength. Wherever a weakness occurs, the body employs another skill to accommodate, adapt, and survive. Just like the rest of the body, the brain operates upon the same principle. This probably seems pretty logical, but for decades the brain has been thought not to possess the same adaptability as the rest of the body.

Part of the reason for this prejudice has simply been that the workings of the mind are mysterious. The body can compensate for a lost limb with other, functional limbs, but should the mind lack the ability to remember well, how can it compensate? People have long assumed memory loss is the inevitable consequence of aging, and when it happens one had better keep a paper and pen on hand at all times, because one's remembering days are over. But neuroplasticity reveals that memory decline is not inevitable, and adults as well as children can indeed improve their memories, as well as all the other cognitive skills, throughout life.[8] Everyone from sufferers of posttraumatic stress disorder, to brain damage victims, to the elderly can benefit from this new knowledge of how to assess, practice, and enrich our amazingly plastic brains. This book, however, is intended to focus solely on how bright children can use the science of neuroplasticity to reach their highest potential with more ease, fun, and love of learning than ever before.

Now that we understand cognitive skills—our ability to memorize, process information, and problem-solve—as the primary pathway by which the plastic, ever-changing brain learns anything it needs to learn, we know that providing a smart child with more information to stuff into his or her brain is not the best way to improve overall scholastic ability, nor even to improve test scores. Instead, educational psychologists today utilize scientifically derived exercises to improve students' basic cognitive skills.

With specific intellectual exercises, people with injured brains can now repair their own neural pathways. Using the same techniques, healthy, bright brains can improve, too. In fact, healthy brains improve in exactly the same way as injured ones: by building massive amounts of neural insulation, called myelin, to ensure the safety and longevity of learned knowledge.[9] Students can build myelin around factual information, such as a list of multiplication tables, but they can also build myelin around the cognitive skills, such as memorization and logic, which enable the brain to more quickly and easily learn and remember those multiplication tables. Working together, neuroplasticity researchers and educational psychologists have developed techniques, first, to assess students as to their current cognitive skills levels, then, to scientifically practice any skills found to be at less than ideal levels, and, finally, to improve those levels. That means students can improve memory, increase problem-solving speed, and achieve mastery of subjects with less overall effort, and more natural joy, than ever before.

Indeed, while improving cognitive skills makes learning easier and more fun for children, it also reduces the stress and pressure associated with advanced academic courses and a competitive school culture. That lower level of stress benefits children immeasurably, but it also benefits you, the parent. You can now leave those flash cards and that stopwatch behind. You can even reduce the tutoring schedule. With help from a trained educational psychologist, your child, within a finite amount of time, can improve his or her cognitive skills in order to get more information out of each class, more fun out of each new learning experience, and, let's not forget that Holy Grail of education: higher test scores.

CHAPTER 3

WHAT'S NEW WITH IQ

Testing in the Age of Neuroplasticity

*Development involves giving up a smaller story
in order to wake up to a larger story.*

JEAN HOUSTON

Parents, students, and teachers alike have, for decades, harbored a love/hate relationship with intelligence quotient (IQ) testing. After all, learning your IQ score feels kind of like getting a palm reading. It's interesting, but you don't want to believe all your life's potential can be summed up so easily. Furthermore, IQ testing has huge educational ramifications. Children who score well on IQ tests, but whose grades don't seem commensurate with their potential, are legally entitled to extra help and enrichment programs in public school. Those who score particularly high often find themselves subject to the stress of high expectations. Conversely, children who score in the low to average range on IQ tests are often not legally entitled to special learning assistance in school. According to educational doctrine, low academic scores, when paired with a low IQ score, is considered the best that child can achieve. But these laws and procedures, though sadly still in place nationwide, are based upon an entirely obsolete model of how the brain works.

Recent research into the science of the human brain has turned the world of intelligence testing on its (pardon the pun) head. We now know that an IQ score, while still a valuable metric, is not the determinate of one's potential it was once thought to be. Instead, this score functions merely as a starting point in a lifelong journey where intelligence and ability are infinitely changeable, or plastic.[10] And, yes, even those with high IQ scores can be helped to succeed further—that means not just getting better grades, but achieving them with more ease, less stress, and greater overall happiness.

Regardless of whether a student's IQ score is high, low, or average, educational psychologists will only be able to use the score to help the child if they know a bit more about the process the brain went through to achieve that score. We get this information by further testing the student's individual cognitive skills. The test results may help us discover, for instance, that a student has achieved a high IQ score mostly by utilizing one extremely acute ability, say visual processing. If so, it is actually possible to help such a student increase his or her auditory processing speed, too, which will add further fuel to the student's intellectual fire. The immediate result is added ease of learning, less stress in school, and higher test scores. In the long term, might such children become the brilliant problem-solvers of tomorrow? I don't see why not. Early testing and appropriate cognitive processing exercises can help students live their entire academic lives at the top of their game.

But why stop with IQ and cognitive skills? It is now possible to test the whole child. That means we can get a baseline score on that child's development in terms of IQ, cognitive skills, social/emotional/behavioral development, speech and language skills, and a few other items—executive functioning, adaptive skills, and processing speed—which I'll talk about in more detail, below. In thinking about testing, it may help to keep in mind that, in many ways, measuring things is a big part of our lives. At the mechanic shop, we measure our vehicle's fluid levels. At the doctor's office, we measure our blood pressure, height, weight, and heart rate. Scientists measure rainfall, pollen counts, and crime rates, while economists measure profits, losses, and changes in markets. These facts and figures help us make important life decisions. So when it comes to our children's brains, does it make any sense to leave things to chance? Deciding to "play it by ear," or "let nature take its course," or "take a wait and see approach" makes sense for a vacation at the seashore but is not a logical attitude for auto maintenance, financial management, scientific inquiry, or a million other aspects of life, including education, where the results are crucial, time-bound, and have long-term effects.

Of course, your child is not a pie graph. Lists of numbers and squiggly lines on a chart will never reveal his or her wonderful personality, loving smile, warm embrace, sense of humor, cute dimples, and adorable eccentricities. The results of these tests are not meant to reduce your beautiful and complex child to numbers and levels and percentiles. They are meant only to help educational psychologists such as myself figure out where hidden difficulties lie so that we can help these ambitious, charismatic beings get the most out of life.

In my work as a school psychologist, I run an extensive battery of tests on my clients; however, most students, in public and private schools alike, will only receive testing in areas where teachers perceive a problem. That is, if they receive any cognitive, social, or emotional testing at all. The best practice is to test children across the board, no matter where they are or are not experiencing difficulties, because testing isn't only intended to find out what's wrong: it is also useful for finding out what's right. The results then enable you, the parent, to guide your child toward ideal study habits and activities.

For instance, should test results show your child is best at auditory processing, you might suggest he or she work in a study group, talk out social problems, and take notes on in-class lectures rather than on assigned reading. Conversely, if your child excels at visual processing, he or she may do better studying alone, taking notes on the reading instead of in-class lectures, and watching documentaries about school subjects. Of course, it is important for a visual processor to increase their auditory processing skills, and vice versa, and we'll talk about how that is done in the next chapter, but there is also no reason not to also take advantage of a natural aptitude for processing certain types of input.

WHAT TESTING MEANS TODAY

By this point you have read the words "test" and "testing" several times, and if you still haven't made the paradigm shift into a full understanding of the findings of neuroplasticity, you might be panicking. After all, parents and educators traditionally have shied away from too much testing, and for good reason. Tests—including IQ tests, achievement tests, psychological tests, and even personality tests—used to be stressful, dreaded events whose outcomes could make or break a student's college choices, employment potential, and even school social status. But now that we know the brain is infinitely plastic, we view IQ and other test scores not as fixed determinates of potential, but as answers to frustrating, long-standing questions, and as a baseline for future development.

After all, when students experience learning disabilities or impairment, typically they know it. Low cognitive skills test results are not the first indicator of academic distress—they're often the last. With these results, which now pinpoint blocks to learning far more specifically than ever before, students finally discover which aspect of their neurological make-up needs a jump start. With determination and the help of a licensed psychologist or neuropsychologist, even long-standing problems can usually be remedied in a matter of weeks.

Many parents will read this chapter on testing with a sense of familiarity. Your high-performing children may already have been through batteries of tests. If so, then you know the usefulness of test results can vary. This is because not every testing process is alike. There are qualified administrators of these tests and unqualified administrators. Did you know a psychologist has to take eight or nine different assessment classes just to become certified to give the most common cognitive tests? Finding a licensed practitioner to administer the battery of tests should be a parent's very first priority, as tests given by unlicensed personnel may be inaccurate and are inadmissible when applying for testing modifications.

For this reason, if your children are being offered cognitive testing through the public school system, be patient and expect to jump through some hoops to get it, but you can expect the tests to be properly administered. If you are using the private sector, check the test administrator's credentials, because improperly administered tests can lead to retests, and excessive testing wastes your child's time. Because private practice tests can be expensive for you, it is important to do the testing right the first time, in order to use those results to best advantage.

THE ROLE OF AN
EDUCATIONAL PSYCHOLOGIST

In my work as an educational psychologist, once I am armed with test results for cognitive skills, processing speed, executive function, and IQ, only then do I take a look at the results of the student's academic achievement tests. If I notice, for instance, that the student's scores in language arts are low, I will look among the other test scores for a clue as to why that might be happening. Perhaps the child has a low visual processing speed, and the teacher in that class relies heavily upon handouts. Or perhaps the student scores lowest, academically, on mathematics. If the logic section of his cognitive test is low, that could explain it. However, if his logic scores are high, along with working memory and executive function, then I know the problem must lie elsewhere. Perhaps a look at the social/emotional side of the spectrum will shed some light on what is going wrong in math class. Because these interlinking factors can all come into play, beginning with a full battery of detailed tests is the best way to help any child succeed.

Public schools tend to test speech and language in preschool, at age two or three, especially if speech does not develop quickly. Schools also tend to test for autism and autism spectrum disorder between the ages three and five. Cognitive skills, processing, social/emotional, and executive function can be tested from age three on up, though I don't always recommend testing before age six, because the attention span is not mature enough yet. The earlier teachers can detect and improve any shortcomings in these areas, the better, both for the child's academic success and his or her self-esteem.

That said, why wait until your child has been suffering for years, never realizing it is possible to read quickly and efficiently, never understanding why it takes him twice as much work to succeed as it takes others? When you test as early as is developmentally reasonable, you can intervene and solve any processing issues so that learning remains always an adventure and never a chore; meanwhile, self-esteem stays high.

As I mentioned above, early testing also enables students and parents to identify the parts of the intellect that are functioning efficiently. This way students can take full advantage of this knowledge by studying in such a way that they activate the most well-developed parts of their brains. I can't overstate the importance of discovering not just what is going wrong in your child's cognitive makeup, but also what is going right.

TESTS YOU MAY ENCOUNTER

Numerous tests exist, covering every brain function under the sun. Each one is designed to test slightly different aspects of a child's learning process, so simply knowing which test to give a student requires your school psychologist or licensed educational psychologist to have a great deal of background knowledge. Just to give you a glimpse into my world, I have listed below the tests we psychologists have to choose from as we help you on your journey toward best-practice education. (Don't worry, there won't be a quiz.)

Cognitive Ability Tests

- Wechsler Intelligence Scale for Children® – Fifth Edition (WISC®-V)
- Wechsler Adult Intelligence Scale – Fourth Edition (WAIS-IV)
- Wechsler Abbreviated Scale of Intelligence™ (WASI™)
- Wechsler Preschool and Primary Scale of Intelligence™ – Fourth Edition (WPPSI™-IV)
- Kaufman Assessment Battery for Children – Third Edition (KABC™-III)
- Differential Ability Scales®-III (DAS-III®)
- Test of Nonverbal Intelligence – Fifth Edition (TONI-5)
- Woodcock-Johnson® III Normative Update (NU)
- Tests of Cognitive Abilities (Cognitive Abilities Scale – Second Edition (CAS-2))
- NEPSY® – Second Edition (NEPSY®-II)

Achievement Tests

- Woodcock-Johnson® IV Normative Update (NU)
- Tests of Achievement, Forms A and B
- Woodcock-Johnson® III Normative Update (NU) Form C/ Brief Battery
- Wechsler Individual Achievement Test® – Third Edition (WIAT®-III)
- BRIGANCE® Comprehensive Inventory of Basic Skills II (CIBS II)
- Gray Oral Reading Test-Fifth Edition (GORT-5)
- Test of Written Language – Fourth Edition (TOWL-4)
- Dyslexia Screening Instrument (DSI)

- Wide Range Achievement Test 5 (WRAT-5)
- Bracken School Readiness Assessment – Third Edition (BSRA-3)

Processing Skills Assessment

- The Beery-Buktenica Developmental Test of Visual-Motor Integration – Sixth Edition (BEERY™ VMI)
- Bender® Visual-Motor Gestalt Test (Bender-Gestalt II)
- Wide Range Assessment of Memory and Learning – Second Edition (WRAML-2)
- Test of Auditory Processing Skills – Third Edition (TAPS-3)
- Comprehensive Test of Phonological Processing – Second Edition (CTOPP-2)
- Stroop Color-Word Test (SCWT)

Social-Emotional-Behavioral Development Tests

- Behavior Assessment System for Children – Second Edition (BASC-3)
- Conners Continuous Performance Test – Third Edition™ (Conners CPT 3™)
- Roberts Apperception Test for Children (Roberts-2)
- Depression and Anxiety in Youth Scale (DAYS)
- Scales for Assessing Emotional Disturbance – Second Edition (SAED-2)
- Gilliam Autism Rating Scale – Third Edition (GARS-3)
- Gilliam Asperger's Disorder Scale (GADS™)
- Autism Diagnostic Observation Schedule™ (ADOS™)
- Attention Deficit Hyperactivity Disorder (ADHD) rating scales
- Attention Deficit Disorder (ADD) rating scales
- Piers-Harris Children's Self-Concept Scale™ – Second Edition (Piers-Harris™ 2)

House-Tree-Person Projective Test

- Beck Anxiety Inventory® (BAI®)

Executive Functioning Tests

- Delis-Kaplan Executive Function System™ (D-KEFS™)
- Behavior Rating Inventory of Executive Function® (BRIEF®)

Adaptive Tests

- Scales of Independent Behavior-Revised (SIB-R)
- Adaptive Behavior Assessment System® – Second Edition (ABAS®-2)
- Vineland Adaptive Behavior Scales – Third Edition (Vineland™-III)

Speech And Language Tests

- Comprehensive Assessment of Spoken Language (CASL™)
- Khan-Lewis Phonological Analysis – Second Edition (KLPA-2)
- Test of Pragmatic Language – Second Edition (TOPL-2)
- Arizona Articulation Proficiency Scale – Third Edition (ARIZONA-3)
- Bankson-Bernthal Test of Phonology (BBTOP)
- Diagnostic Evaluation of Articulation and Phonology (DEAP)
- Kaufman Speech Praxis Test (KSPT)
- Super Duper® Preschoolers Acquiring Language Skills (PALS) and (PALS-2)

Whether you are talking to a school guidance counselor, educational or school psychologist, or private educational company, you will want to ask what tests they intend to use to determine your child's baseline. (I'll talk more about what a baseline is, below.) Don't worry, you don't need to know each and every test listed above, but it does help to understand that a full battery of tests includes one, and sometimes two, tests from each category (excluding the adaptive and speech and language categories, except under special circumstances).

Many educational resource companies administer the cognitive and academic tests; however, their results can be invalid due to the fact that cognitive assessments may only be legally administered by a licensed psychologist. Therefore, an independently practicing, licensed psychologist is, in many cases, the best professional to turn to in order to get the full battery of tests.

HOW TO USE THE TEST RESULTS

Once you have a full battery of test results on file, you have two incredible advantages. First, you have a baseline for remediating the problematic areas. In other words, you know where to start working and from what point to measure future progress. Second, if children score below average and show a gap between cognition and academics, they are very likely to be legally entitled to extra time on the SAT and ACT tests. This benefit is something you have every right to take advantage of. Keep in mind, the fact that your child had extra time on these tests will remain completely confidential, forever. No college admissions officer will ever know about it. With that in mind, you owe it to your children to have their cognitive skills tested! Getting extra time on an SAT or ACT test is just one of many huge advantages that a battery of tests can offer bright, ambitious children.

If test scores show that your child is entitled to extra time on the SAT or ACT, assure him or her it is nothing of which to be ashamed. This is all confidential information, which can and should remain confidential. This means that no one in college admissions will know your child got extra time on the SAT or the ACT. Once your child is admitted to the college, then you can share the report so that he or she can benefit if accommodations are needed. This information is confidential for a reason. Anyway, since you are a smart parent, you are going to go ahead and have a licensed educational psychologist work with your child to bring those cognitive skills up to average, above average, or even to a superior level. I have done this, and seen it done, hundreds of times, because, as I have said many times and will continually remind you: brainpower is not fixed, but plastic.

Children diagnosed with specific learning disabilities also may take advantage of supplementary educational opportunities, either through a special education designation or, better yet, through a 504 plan, which enables children to receive help for their impairments while participating in regular classes. If, as a parent, you suspect your child may have attention deficit, autism, or some other learning disability, you might hesitate to have him or her tested for fear of receiving a damning diagnosis, but, remember, this is the age of neuroplasticity. Your hesitation is based upon an obsolete model of how the brain works. Today the test results can only help you.

Getting a baseline for your child's ADHD, dyslexia, dyspraxia, auditory processing disorder, autism spectrum disorder, or any other less-than-ideal cognitive function simply provides you with a place to start in remediating your child's particular cognitive-processing issue. Why wait? Test as soon as possible, so you and a licensed psychologist can start your child down the road to academic excellence as soon as possible.

PROFESSIONALS WHO CAN HELP YOU

If, in the course of their academic lives, students experience any learning difficulties at all, they are likely to encounter some of the following individuals: teachers or advisors, social workers, educational specialists or therapists, speech and language specialists or therapists, occupational therapists, college and vocational counselors, school counselors, clinical psychologists, licensed educational psychologists, school psychologists, neuropsychologists, psychometrists, psychiatrists, and physicians. Let's talk about exactly what type of help you can expect from each of these professionals.

All of the above individuals can give academic tests; however, only some of them are qualified to diagnose learning disabilities. Others use their expertise to simply raise the question, then refer the child to a specialist for a definitive diagnosis. There have been innumerable instances of diagnoses performed by unqualified personnel leading struggling students down the wrong path to remediation while wasting precious time, energy, and money, so always ask for the administrator's qualifications before investing in tests, diagnoses, or remediation.

COGNITIVE ASSESSMENTS

The following professionals are qualified to administer cognitive tests:

- Clinical psychologists
- School psychologists (in a school setting)
- Licensed educational psychologists (in school setting or in private practice)
- Psychometrists
- Psychiatrists
- Neuropsychologists

The following professionals are *not* qualified to administer cognitive tests: school counselors, vocational counselors, social workers, speech and language specialists, occupational therapists, education specialists or therapists, or physicians. However, these professionals may be part of a diagnostic team and can offer valuable input.

EDUCATION PROFESSIONALS AND THEIR QUALIFICATIONS/LICENSES

	Qualified to administer psycho-educational assessments	Qualified to diagnose students from DSM-V	Qualified to prescribe medication for ADHD	Licensed provider
Clinical psychologist	Yes	Yes	No	Yes
School psychologist in a school setting	Yes	Yes	No	Yes, but only if credentialed
Licensed Educational Psychologist (LEP) in private practice	Yes	Yes	No	Yes
Psychometrist	Yes	Yes	No	Yes
Psychiatrist	No	Yes	Yes	Yes
Neuropsychologist	Yes	Yes	No	Yes
School counselor	No	No	No	No
Vocational counselor	No	No	No	No
Mental health counselor	No	Yes	No	Yes
Social worker	No Social/ emotional only	Yes	No	Yes
Speech and language specialist	No Speech test only	No, unless disability pertains to speech and language	No	Yes, if in private practice
Occupational therapist	No Occupational therapy tests only	No, unless disability pertains to occupational therapy	No	Yes, if in private practice
Education therapist	No Academic tests only	No	No	No
Physician	No	Yes	Yes	Yes
Marriage and family therapist	No Social/ emotional tests only	Yes	No	Yes

LEARNING DISABILITIES

Once a student has taken the tests, the next step is to diagnose any learning disabilities that may have been found in order to qualify him or her for benefits such as school programs, a 504 plan, and extra time on the SAT or ACT. The following professionals are qualified to use test results to diagnose learning disabilities:

- Clinical psychologists
- School psychologists (in a school setting)
- Licensed educational psychologists (in private practice)
- Neuropsychologists
- Psychometrists
- Physicians

The following professionals are *not* qualified to diagnose your child with a learning disability, although, of course, their input will be valued within any diagnostic team: educational therapists, school counselors, vocational counselors, social workers, occupational therapists (unless the learning disability pertains to occupational therapy), and speech and language specialists (unless the disability is speech or language based).

If you and your child decide to add medication for ADHD to your remediation program, only the following individuals can prescribe it:

- Psychiatrists
- Physicians

SOCIAL/EMOTIONAL TESTING

The following professionals are qualified to conduct tests under the social/emotional category. They can also assess, diagnose, and provide therapy for emotional problems.

- Clinical psychologists
- School psychologists (in school setting)

- Psychometrists
- Social workers
- Psychiatrists
- Licensed educational psychologists (private practice)
- Marriage and family therapists
- Mental health counselors

Parents of today's students might remember the 1970s television show *The Six Million Dollar Man*, and the show's opening catch phrase, "We can rebuild him. We have the technology." Back then, the idea was science fiction, but now we do have the technology, perhaps not to rebuild exactly, but certainly to coach each student to improve, perhaps even beyond his wildest dreams. And by technology, I'm not talking about nuts and bolts or lasers and microchips. Instead, all one needs to improve students' cognitive skills are a pencil and paper, a few pieces of playground equipment, and one highly trained school psychologist, licensed educational psychologist, or neuropsychologist. Using today's understanding of cognitive skills, memory, processing speed, and executive functions, and the revelations of neuroplasticity, we can train the brain to do, then to master, and finally to enjoy the tasks it has trained itself to avoid in order to prevent failure.

CHAPTER 4

THE BRAIN TRAINING PROCESS

Coaching Students to Become their Best

*The key is not the will to win... Everybody has that.
It is the will to prepare to win that is important.*

BOBBY KNIGHT

uilding skill or knowledge of any kind is, of course, a multi-step process. Cognitive skills practice will significantly improve students' abilities to learn and retain information, but then, of course, the students must apply those abilities by practicing the skill, or studying the knowledge, they seek. This is another area where the findings of neuroplasticity help us. Let's take a look at what neuroscientists now consider the ideal method of practice or study, and then we'll talk about how improving cognitive skills can enhance such efforts.

DEEP PRACTICE

Well-meaning parents often urge their children to study and practice their various subjects, instruments, sports, and skills every day, with varying results. Sometimes these hard-working students turn out to be virtuosos, geniuses, and leaders in their fields, but other times they grow to resent the constant impetus to work, the exhaustion, and the sense of being on an educational treadmill. Which of these results is achieved has more to do with the student's methods of independent study and practice than the sheer number of hours put in.

Many well-read parents are aware of the notion that students require ten thousand hours of practice at any skill in order to master it. This finding actually dates all the way back to 1899, but it was officially validated in the late 1970s by psychologist K. Anders Ericsson.[11]

Psychologist Daniel Coyle has recently given us further insight on the subject of mastery; most notably, we now know that when students study and practice their skills correctly, they achieve more in fewer hours, while also requiring more hours of rest, than previously realized. For his 2009 book, *The Talent Code*, Coyle traveled the globe, investigating hotspots of genius in everything from mathematics to soccer. In the process, he came to understand that ten thousand hours of practice are not necessarily enough to gain mastery. In fact, students must also utilize the right type of practice. Coyle went on to codify the type of practice that appears to lead, across the board, to mastery of any skill. He calls it "deep practice."[12]

In a way, deep practice is quite simple. For some students, the skill comes naturally, while for others it may require an unusual level of concentration. Regardless, its efficacy is indisputable. It consists of the following basic steps:

1. Practice the skill—be it chess or ballet, tennis or mathematics—until you commit an error or encounter a problem.
2. Stop. Solve the problem or examine the error. Different pursuits will entail different methods for doing this, but the key is that the student stop whenever an error occurs and puzzle out the reason for the error. Once the cause is found and the error is corrected, the student may return to his or her general practice until the next error occurs.
3. Repeat steps one and two until exhausted
4. Rest.

This simple recipe for success comes with a caveat that boosts achievement even further: if possible, condense the activity so that more errors occur in a shorter time, as each error solved leads the student toward mastery. For instance, Brazilian soccer players refine their skills in a small practice room, not out on the field, and master skateboarders have been known to practice inside empty swimming pools, where they can repeatedly confront the most challenging angles pavement has to offer.[13]

Step four, above, is also extremely important. When utilizing deep practice, students will tire more quickly. Coyle reveals that whereas some students can practice for eight hours a day, those utilizing the deep practice method will tire after only two or three and get more benefit from their work.[14] So, yes, the benchmark for mastery is still ten thousand hours, but these are deep practice hours, which can only be practiced a few at a time and must be followed by adequate rest. Any way you look at it, there is simply no rushing genius.

TEACHING VERSUS COACHING

Coyle's codification of deep practice meshes perfectly with recent discoveries in both our understanding of neuroplasticity and our ability to test cognitive skills. To wit: if the quality of concentration utilized during practice time is of paramount importance (and clearly it is), then if we can improve our cognitive skills (memory, attention, pattern identification, and auditory and visual processing), we will indeed get more out of each and every hour of practice and even find those hours of deep practice more enjoyable and fulfilling. This means less nagging from parents and more self-motivation from students.

With neuroplasticity telling us it is indeed possible to improve our brains, and research into cognitive skills telling us exactly how to measure the levels of the brain's various skills, it remains only to explain how exactly educational psychologists set about achieving just that. In short, we guide students through a customized series of practice sessions designed to ever-so-gradually improve a cognitive skill. The work entails simply testing to determine a starting point, practicing the skill at ever-increasing levels of difficulty, and finally improving the skill—often beyond the students' wildest dreams—then retesting for confirmation of success. This process may seem rather ordinary, but, remember, we are not practicing for a spelling bee, nor memorizing pi; we are working on cognitive skills, which are essential brain functions, so these practice sessions involve creative, unusual, and highly personalized methods.

After receiving my neuropsychology assessment certificate from UC Berkeley, I simply couldn't get enough of neuroplasticity. I read every book on the subject and felt amazed to finally have a confirmation of something I had felt all along: before working with a teacher, a child should first work with a great coach. In basketball, the coach is the one who drills the students in layups and free-throws, pushes them to improve footwork and shooting skills, and takes note of a wrong twist of the shoulder or an off-balance stance, ensuring players' basic skills are up to par. Later, during a game, the coach acts as a teacher, setting up plays to be performed and winning strategies to execute. Without the initial practice in fundamentals, the players would never be able to execute such plays, but a team that is well-drilled on fundamentals finds winning easy.

In academics, cognitive skills form the fundamentals of learning. Whereas teachers have, from time immemorial, drilled students on their multiplication tables and spelling words, neuroscience (and my basketball analogy) says this is putting the game before the practice. In order to succeed at a level of ease that initiates a true joy of learning, students must first enhance the cognitive skills of memory, logic, and visual and auditory processing. Understanding this, when I worked as school psychologist at Cate School, I found it a natural next step to develop cognitive skills drills for children that would utilize the principles of neuroplasticity. Thus was born the educational remediation and acceleration program I call BrainMatterZ.

I'll provide more details on BrainMatterZ below, but first, to be fair, I must tell you I was not the first person to invent a cognitive skills training program. Educators on the fringes have been toying with the idea of helping students improve their cognitive skills for years. Numerous computer programs are now available to aid people of all ages in improving their cognitive functioning. Also, innumerable professionals—from psychologists to school counselors to life coaches—now claim to be able to test and improve students' cognitive skills.

As both an English teacher and a special education teacher, I saw many bright students go through such programs, as well as numerous tutoring and subject-matter-specific acceleration programs, with varying degrees of success. As any neuroscientist could predict, the tutoring programs provided some of the students with limited advances in test scores in their specific fields; however, they did not put smiles on the students' faces or cause them to look forward to class every day, nor were they intended to have such far-reaching results.

Among the students utilizing cognitive skills enhancement computer programs, I also found some advances in test scores and overall academic performance, but the advances were short-lived, largely because other things—such as low confidence levels, social awkwardness, and distractions—often trumped academic knowledge when it came to test-day success. In addition, there is some question as to whether cognitive skills enhanced through a digitized computer model transfer into real-life and actual paper-and-pencil, test-taking skills. The research on this issue, which psychologists call transference, has so far been inconclusive.[15]

With my coaching background, I know first-hand how big a difference a supportive, team-oriented social setting can make to a child's learning process and personal development. That's why, as a teacher, while I understand computers play an important role in education, I have never been a fan of them being used as a central learning tool. Since I think of teaching as coaching, and a classroom as a court where students work together to rebound that ball and sink it deep in the academic basket, I can't fathom a computer classroom where all the children face away from each other and the teacher, immerse themselves in digitized worlds of their own, and cut out all the unpredictable, risky, funny, enlightening, and bonding experiences provided by an interactive group setting.

To me (and to famed educational theorists Jean Piaget and Lev Vygotsky) learning is a social activity.[16] The whole child simply cannot grow in a non-social setting, and, much to the disappointment of the franchised tutoring companies out there, children's minds can not be programmed like computers. My ongoing attempt to achieve the same goals as an educational psychologist that I achieved as a coach—using a coach's highly social, encouraging, fundamentals-based approach—led me to experiment with the findings of neuroplasticity. Thus I founded BrainMatterZ, my approach to cognitive skills enhancement in a positive, encouraging, and always-interactive setting.

CASE STUDY: GARY

One of my first BrainMatterZ students, Gary, came to me in the fifth grade. A bright student from an education-positive home, he had become highly discouraged by a lifelong difficulty with reading. In fact, he got headaches when he read, so he tended to avoid homework at any cost. His concerned parents brought him to me, telling me their son wouldn't crack a book unless one of them stood by, constantly encouraging and offering incentives. They had tried tutoring and computerized brain-enhancement programs, but Gary simply didn't have the wherewithal to show up regularly and stay focused on these activities.

First, I put Gary through a battery of initial tests. I liken these tests to junior varsity tryouts. Think of how, on that first day of tryouts, players do wind sprints, shoot baskets, and play defensive drills while the coach takes notes on their skills and abilities. Contrary to what many players imagine, as a coach at tryouts, I'm not looking for superstars, but simply determining who will need help in which aspect of fundamentals. I want a team that can cover the court for both offense and defense and that has the emotional fortitude to handle a referee's bad call with grace. Most of all, I want a team that communicates and knows how to work together. Since no players get cut from junior varsity tryouts, this event isn't a pass-fail test. It's a positive, encouraging environment where I promote the advantages of joining a sports team.

In the same way, I utilized Gary's initial battery of tests only to set our starting point and determine benchmarks for improvement. This is what is meant by a "baseline." Once tabulated, Gary's test results helped me ascertain that although he had superior verbal and auditory system processing, his fluid intelligence and visual processing speed were low.

In layman's language, that means Gary could learn from a teacher's in-class lectures and respond to in-class questions, but when it came to reading, copying information off the blackboard, or remembering elements of seen words or pictures, he fell short. "Fluid intelligence" simply refers to the student's ability to reason quickly and think abstractly. It is the kind of intelligence useful in making snap decisions in the middle of playing a sport, driving on a busy interstate, or playing chess. The ability to think abstractly covers a lot of brain functions, most notably the utilization of symbols, such as musical notes or mathematical symbols, to represent real-world things or concepts.

Just as skills in free-throws, layups, offense, and defense all need to be present for a team to win, the full range of cognitive skills must also be present inside a student's brain for optimal success. Luckily, the brain already understands teamwork. Often, when a student works hard to improve auditory processing skills, visual processing skills will also improve. Attention and memory may improve as well. That means working on cognitive skills is, quite literally, like cross-training for the brain.

After giving Gary the full battery of tests, I shared the results with him, ensuring that he understood all news was good news. Gary had never viewed testing in this way before. A low test score still meant failure to him. Gary hadn't yet fully grasped the paradigm shift brought about by neuroplasticity and science's current understanding of cognitive skills. To help the concept sink in, I reminded Gary that we already knew he had certain processing issues, but these tests enabled us to learn exactly what those issues were. Now I could help him by addressing the issues, one by one. Best of all, the test results explained why Gary couldn't concentrate on reading and gave us a way to fix that problem.

Finally, Gary made the paradigm shift from seeing test results as damning grades to seeing them as answers to questions he had long been asking, like, "Why can't I concentrate on reading?"

"The answer," I told him, "is because your visual processing speed needs work. So, let's get to work, shall we?"

He smiled at that. "Get to work. Solve the problem. Yes, let's."

In the past, when coaching players through basketball drills, I understood that these exercises should challenge the player just enough to engage the brain, but not enough to frustrate. After all, an over-challenged player who can't succeed might throw down the ball and stalk off to the locker room, ready to give up. Emotions come to the forefront when students feel over-challenged, yet the brain does not engage when the challenge is not great enough. Finding that sweet spot was, and still is, the key to both coaching sports and building cognitive skills with BrainMatterZ.

To engage Gary's brain's visual processing apparatus, I further broke down this skill into the components of horizontal and vertical tracking. To engage his horizontal tracking, I created a worksheet with dozens of pairs of words down the left side, in a column. The column on the right side of the page contained only ten individual words. I assigned Gary to ascertain, as quickly as possible, whether any of the words in the right-hand column were repeated in the left-hand column. In an exercise like this, similar words, like "eat" and "heat" might throw off a student with poor visual processing, but those pairs are easy enough to identify when a student slows down and paces himself.

This and another worksheet—so arranged that it necessitated Gary comparing items at the top and bottom of each page, to engage vertical tracking—constituted Gary's visual processing practice. With a few hours' practice, Gary mastered these drills, so next I timed him, just to keep the challenge high. At this point, he finally understood that the stopwatch's results follow the same rule as the battery of tests—they simply gave us a starting point and something for which to strive. They didn't determine anything fixed about his mental powers.

Once Gary could consistently beat his own time, improving visual processing speed with each exercise, I added one more challenge: distraction. I asked Gary what kind of music he hated more than anything in the world. He laughed and told me, "Country Western!" So, much to his horror, I asked him to do the visual processing exercises, while still trying to beat his old time, but this time with country music softly humming, then playing, then blasting in the background. When he mastered that, I added the distraction of myself babbling loudly and nonsensically in the background. Then I rattled a drawer full of pencils and pens while singing along, off-key, at the top of my voice, to the hated music. Still Gary concentrated. Okay, he laughed now, but he managed to concentrate in spite of it all. He beat his own time at the visual processing exercises, and we actually had some fun along with it.

I feel our laughing together and our friendly interaction throughout the process provided a much-needed social element to the program. Neuroscience states that the brain doesn't operate in isolation, it needs social interaction as well as intellectual stimulation. That means that trying to engage the brain academically and non-socially (which is what computerized brain-enhancement programs do) doesn't access the whole brain and leaves the student, after a great deal of effort, with less than ideal results.

By confronting Gary with a condensed version of the task he found difficult and then ever-so-gradually increasing its difficulty level, I was able to help him train his brain to overcome all the issues that had once plagued him. In the not-so-distant past, no educator nor psychologist would even have tried such an approach, due to the pervasive belief in fixed intelligence. But now we know better. Little by little, any student's shortcoming can be improved. The key is in approaching the problem very specifically and slowly increasing the difficulty level.

The work I did with Gary showed results very quickly. He completed twelve hours of brain training that summer and returned the two following summers for boosters, just to keep his skills in shape. He went on to show marked improvement in a follow-up battery of tests before gaining admittance to, and excelling at, a rigorous high school. After the initial twelve hours of work with me, his verbal comprehension went from a high average score to very superior. His perceptual reasoning went from low-average to high-average, and his working memory index progressed from average to very superior. Best yet, Gary's processing speed progressed from an initial score of borderline to very superior. When I saw that, I knew BrainMatterZ was on the right track.

CASE STUDY: BARBARA

Not all students can improve their cognitive skills merely with paper-and-pencil worksheets. Students present with a wide variety of processing issues, some of which require more complex remediation. Let's take a look at another student, Barbara. A junior in high school, Barbara came to me complaining of finding school increasingly difficult. She was a hard-working, serious student with a high IQ, but these days, homework took longer to do than ever before, and she didn't understand why. After putting her through a full battery of tests, I discovered the cause of her problem. Although Barbara had very high verbal comprehension, her processing speed was in the low average range, and her perceptual reasoning and working memory were only average. When paired with a high IQ, these are exactly the kind of disparities that cause a child to feel incredibly frustrated.

Barbara needed to work on both auditory and visual processing speeds as well as working memory in order to bring up that low processing speed, so the next time she came into my office, I surprised her with an unusual task. I asked Barbara to stand on a balance board and hold a beanbag in her right hand. (A balance board is like a small teeter-totter that you stand on with both feet. The child is challenged to balance on the wobbling board without either side touching the ground.) I told Barbara that her right hand represented odd numbers, and the left, even numbers. Then I instructed her to toss the beanbag from right to left and count by twos while the beanbag was in the air.

"Two, four, six, eight," she said, deftly tossing and catching the bag.

Then I told her that when tossing from left to right, she would count by odd numbers.

"One, three, five," she said, tossing the beanbag back to the right.

"Now," I said. "Do you remember where you were on the even numbers? You ended on eight. So toss from right to left again, starting with eight and counting up by evens."

"Eight, ten, twelve, fourteen," she said, correcting her stance on the board and catching the bag in her left hand.

Next she had to remember where she had left off with the odd numbers and count up by odds as she tossed the bag from left to right.

This exercise requires the student to remember information that she says and hears only, so it exercises memory and processing speed as related to auditory, not visual perception. The balance board adds an extra bit of challenge, but it actually helps the student succeed by forcing her to concentrate with her whole self. That extra level of difficulty increases the type of concentration needed for deep practice.

When Barbara achieved a certain level of success with the exercise, to further complicate matters I told her that if she misremembered the starting place for either sequence, she had to start over at the beginning, but just for that sequence. So, while the odds continued to climb higher, the evens ended up going back to the beginning, and the number sequences grew increasingly differentiated from one another. Later, to further increase the difficulty, I asked her to count down from the odd numbers and up with the evens. Finally, after many hours of practice, I added the elements of timing and distraction, just as I had done with Gary, to ensure that Barbara's improved cognitive ability remained true under any circumstance.

This exercise trains memory and auditory processing along with kinesthetic processing—learning by doing. Combining activities like this helps a great deal because of the brain's incredible cross-training powers. Simply training one skill, such as auditory processing, can actually help another skill, such as visual processing, go up. No one quite knows why. But in this case, we trained several types of processing at once, which is known to have even more far-reaching effects.

This type of training is similar to a basketball player running a circuit where she shoots layups, runs wind sprints, practices defensive maneuvers, shoots free-throws, then repeats the circuit. Improving skill at each one of these activities will actually help a player with all of them as a whole. Using these and other exercises to train her cognitive skills over sessions amounting to thirty-six hours, Barbara brought that low-average processing speed up to high-average, her working memory up from average to very superior, and her perceptual reasoning up from average to high-average. Interestingly, her IQ also shot up from high-average to superior. This is an example of the effects of cross-training.

I have used that same method of building from worksheet or activity, to stopwatch, to background noise, to audacious, in-your-face distractions with many students since Gary and Barbara, and, at the end, students always tell me the same thing:

"Dr. Linzey,

Without you shaking pencils in my face and that horrible music blasting away, taking the SAT test was actually fun!"

Another aspect of BrainMatterZ that really encourages students is the fact that, with this being one-on-one training, they get their results right away. If a student didn't beat last week's score on a timed activity, she will know immediately and often beg for another chance. Typical of high-achieving, charismatic students, many of my clients feel a great deal of self-motivation to beat that score. Immediate feedback naturally motivates self-starting students to try harder.

Drills like the visual-processing ones I assigned Gary not only improve students' test-taking abilities but also their ability to concentrate on, and get the most out of, reading a book. At the end of a particularly good session, I tell my students to go home and pick up the daily newspaper or a novel. Read a paragraph. See how it feels. Invariably they have increased their fluency, speed, and ability. Amazed by the results, they often tell me they just never realized that reading could be like this. They had become so accustomed to it being difficult, they never knew other people had a different experience.

These same types of exercises work for students and adults with dyslexia and other severe visual and auditory processing issues. Being plastic, the brain can grow and overcome processing impairments, but it takes concentrated effort and know-how, and these efforts must be undertaken under certain conditions. BrainMatterZ achieves this utilizing the principles of identifying each individual issue, addressing them in isolation, and gradually increasing the difficulty level—not on a computer, but in a real-world setting with an educational psychologist constantly offering encouraging words and praise. This non-computerized, interactive setting means students and parents never have to worry about whether or not these hard-won skills will transfer to schoolwork and other real-world settings.

CHAPTER 5

BRINGING YOUR "A" GAME

How Happiness Affects Learning

*The happiness of your life depends upon
the quality of your thoughts.*

MARCUS AURELIUS, *MEDITATIONS*

While designing BrainMatterZ, I utilized every bit of scientific research I could find on neuroplasticity, the science of happiness, and the science of performance. After all, in school, just as in sports, many factors besides cognitive skills come into play. Coaches often say that certain players may not have great skills, but they "have heart." This means a player is self-motivated to learn, brings a positive attitude on and off the court, and never gives up. These are the non-prima-donna players who give pep talks to fellow players, help others without being asked, and never say die, even if the team loses game after game. While "having heart" is not a cognitive skill, it is crucial to academics, the game of basketball, and, dare I say, the game of life. When players bring heart to a basketball team, they basically bring a certain level of indefatigable happiness that rubs off on other players. Some may argue that happiness is bred by success, that a winning team will contain more players with heart than a losing one, but science actually tells us the opposite is true. Intrinsically happy players (and students) make a team (or academic career) successful, not the other way around.

Traditionally, parents encourage students to think big because we feel success will lead to their ultimate happiness. After all, an Ivy League degree should prepare a student for a high-paying job, which should enable him or her to support a family in style, which should amount to a great adult life. In fact, in many education-driven subcultures, people instinctively believe that happiness is something to postpone until after college graduation; then, sometimes, until after achieving financial success; and then, sometimes, until after raising one's children; and then, ultimately, until retirement. Taking this long view of the philosophy, a certain absurdity appears.

We all know that we must decide, at some point, that in order to be happy, we have to prioritize the things that make us happy. But when should we choose activities oriented towards long-term satisfaction versus those that give us short-term pleasure? In their own ways, children ask parents this difficult question all the time. Sometimes students want to relax, but they worry about falling behind in their academics. Some children even work themselves into a state of anxiety, simply because they don't know when to stop studying. The consequences of living an unbalanced life in that regard can be serious. For instance, some high-achievers fail to take time to learn and practice the social skills they will need later in life. In order to help our children learn healthy methods of prioritizing, let's look to science.

Studies show boosting our general happiness is the best way to make us, and our children, not only more successful, but healthier, more creative, and more active and energetic. Scientists came to this conclusion by changing the way they conducted psychological studies: instead of focusing on depression and its causes, they instead sought out exceptionally happy research subjects to discover how they got that way. The research concluded that inherently happy people tend to become successful; however, successful people do not necessarily become happy. This discovery should change everything in terms of how parents and children prioritize. Just like with the discovery that IQ is plastic, we must now make a major paradigm shift in how we view the relationship between success and happiness.

During the studies, researchers defined happiness as "a positive mood in the present and a positive outlook for the future,"[17] and they based their conclusions upon surveys that calculated peoples' individual ratings of their own happiness. In researching happy subjects, these scientists even identified the activities and ways of being that contributed most to overall happiness. Here they are:

- pursuing meaningful life goals
- scanning the world for opportunities
- cultivating an optimistic and grateful mindset
- holding onto rich social relationships
- enjoying momentary blips of positivity

Using these findings as a guide, we can see that inherent happiness, and therefore long-term success, hinges equally upon things like family mealtimes, the camaraderie inherent in playing sports, scoring well on academic exams, meditation or prayer, laughing with friends and associates, and simple things like receiving compliments, gifts, and appreciation.

Understanding that happiness leads to success should make us reconsider the order in which we do things. For instance, sometimes parents give children rewards for hard work and academic accomplishments, the idea being that students work harder when they know it will pay off. However, when it comes to high-achieving, self-motivated students, the biggest payoff is usually a feeling of inner satisfaction. In other words, high-achievers are self motivated because their work is intrinsically meaningful to them. This corresponds to "pursuing meaningful life goals," one of the precursors to happiness mentioned above, so these students already travel the right road to success. Yet, as parents, we still see room for improvement and want to help. In this case, according to the research, the best way to help students is actually to reward them *before* a big test, not after. Research shows that even a simple gift of candy given prior to a task tends to increase happiness enough to improve performance in everyone from doctors to business managers to monks and nuns.[18]

The same research also shows that increased happiness leads to improved physical health. So in order to have healthy, successful children, we must first focus on having happy children. I can hear you all muttering, now: "Easier said than done!" After all, don't all babies cry? Don't all toddlers throw tantrums? Don't all children pout? And aren't all teenagers miserable by nature? Yes, yes, yes, and yes. Yet research-based science actually does give us infallible (drug-free) methods by which to improve happiness (and therefore success) in ourselves and others.

The first method is meditation. This calming mental exercise involves little more than sitting and observing one's breath go in and out of one's body. Meditation is nonjudgmental, in that one does not bother to gauge whether or not one's breath is going in and out at a proper rate. This lack of analysis and assessment, this momentary acceptance of "things just as they are," relaxes the body and mind immeasurably. Many spiritual and religious practices also employ meditative aspects in their rituals. By the same token, these rituals should be beneficial as well. The calming effect of meditation (much like the calming effect of massage or hot-tubbing or snuggling with a loved one) produces dopamine, a chemical precursor to happiness.

Not satisfied with simply determining that meditation leads to financial and personal success, scientists, of course, asked why. Such queries led to a theory called "Broaden and Build[19]," which stands in contrast to the well-known fight-or-flight theory. Fight-or- flight states that fear-based negative emotions produce a chemical reaction that, in order to ensure our physical survival, narrow our viewpoint until the only options we see are fighting the adversary or fleeing the vicinity. We temporarily loose our verbal, reasoning, and logical abilities. In other words, when an organism fears for its physical safety, it concentrates all its energy on the simplest aspects of survival.

By contrast, broaden-and-build states that when we feel positive emotions, which bring on the release of natural chemicals such as serotonin, dopamine, and endorphins, the mind is able to process a broader range of possibilities, leading to more creativity and thoughtfulness. Processing in this manner inevitably engenders more gregarious behavior, thus helping us build more intellectual, social, and physical resources to rely upon for future survival.

Even a simple thing like having something to look forward to can raise happiness levels. Research shows that the *anticipation* of a pleasurable event is an integral part of the happiness that the event provides. So parents can help children improve their academic performance by suggesting pleasant excursions to take place in the future, writing those things on the calendar, and then following through. While we know that treats and rewards offered immediately give a quick boost to the happiness levels of the recipient, it is also true that having something to look forward to does the same thing. Interestingly, there is no research suggesting that happiness is further increased by having the long-term event be a reward contingent upon some kind of achievement. It is actually the anticipation of the event, not the sense of having earned it, that promotes surges in happiness-generating endorphins.

Studies also show that those who surround themselves with positive messages, images, and information sources tend to be happier. While it may seem responsible to stay abreast of every crime and mishap in your city, too much awareness of such negative inputs can reduce your happiness while not actually improving your knowledge of how the world works. In fact, studies show that those who expose themselves to less hard news actually turn out to be better judges of life's natural risks and rewards than those who watch the nightly news on a regular basis.[20] Simple acts such as surrounding oneself with photos of family and friends, speaking in an encouraging way to one another, taking regular breaks from work or study, and periodically getting out into nature, can actually create an ongoing positive-feeling boost that keeps its recipients functioning at higher happiness levels than workaholics who don't take time to smell the roses.

In fact, scientist and business consultant Marcial Losada, who spent a decade researching work teams performing at both high and low levels, determined, through extensive mathematical modeling, that in order for a corporate team to become success-ful it had to meet or exceed a ratio of 2.9013 positive interactions, experiences, and expressions, to every one negative interaction. His studies show that when positive to negative interactions measure in at a ratio of approximately three to one, teams tend to be successful. Dipping below that point, performance consist-ently suffers, and rising above that point, especially up to the ideal ratio of six to one, teams produce peak-level work.[21]

Granted, these results reflect research conducted on adults in business-oriented environments, not on students in schools; however, it seems logical to apply these results across the board. The implications of Losada's lengthy study couldn't be more clear: people respond well to positivity—such as compliments, encouragement, and good news—and are not motivated by neg-ativity—such as threats, reprimands, and news of disaster. Even in the military, more rewards tend to be awarded to squadrons whose leaders are openly encouraging, while the lowest per-forming teams tend to be led by negative, controlling, and aloof commanders.[22] Negativity may be traditional in the military (and many academic environments as well); however, science now shows that this management style is not conducive to achieving superior results.

Of course, researchers can tell us what behaviors bring results, but they can't make it easy for us to achieve them. We ourselves must figure out how to make this game-changing infor-mation work for us. Learning to switch from negative to positive ways of thinking and speaking, and finding ways to surround your family with positive expressions and experiences, will cer-tainly take effort and creativity. The study does not imply that parents, managers, or commanders shouldn't express anger and negative feelings (sometimes you just have to let it out!), it merely cautions us to keep in mind that all-important, three-to-one ratio.

Another method for improving happiness includes doing activities that exercise a signature strength. This is why small children love to read the same storybooks over and over. They become experts in reading these books, and reading and reread-ing them allows the children to exercise that strength. In addition to learned skills, people also have strengths of character—such as being a good listener, the life of the party, or a helpful handy-man. Exercising these signature strengths, especially if they have not been exercised in a while, brings a flood of positive emotions and boosts happiness. So if you know your child is good at some-thing, whether it be building banana splits or solving equations, why not suggest he or she take time out from less immediately rewarding pursuits to do that certain something that guarantees success and a sense of well-being? The happiness earned from a "signature strength break" can help your child ace a test, impress a teacher, or solve a difficult problem.

Committing "conscious acts of kindness" is another proven technique for creating a happiness surge that can last for days. Science shows that acts of simple helpfulness or altruism tend to produce positive feelings in the giver as well as the receiver. According to research, the best bet for ensuring your altruistic endeavors do the trick is to pile them on. For instance, a study showed that when people consciously performed five kind and helpful acts within a twenty-four-hour period, their happiness levels remained far higher than a control group who performed no such acts, and this difference lasted for several days. Many schools now integrate social service into their curricula in order to teach students the value of community involvement. In so doing, they also teach students to consciously act for the good of another, sometimes while also exercising a signature strength, which ought to give their happiness, therefore their likelihood of both short- and long-term success, a massive boost.

Scientists have even codified how one should spend one's money in order to achieve the greatest happiness advantage.

Contrary to popular belief, studies show that purchasing desired objects and products tends to give fleeting pleasure at best, while investing in events and experiences, especially with other people, brings long-lasting happiness.[23] It makes sense: when we want to feel happy, we often return, in our minds, to pleasant memories, so what could boost happiness better than doing the things that create those memories? To boost happiness even further, scientists say people should spend money on others. This prosocial spending (also known as: the drinks are on me!) is actually proven to make people happier, at the end of the day, than if they had spent the same amount of money on themselves.

Exercise also has long been known to boost endorphins. Studies show that, over both the short and long term, exercise of any kind, even if it is practiced sporadically, helps alleviate depression better than medication. With this in mind, parents can help students succeed by encouraging participation in sports, nature hikes, dancing, bicycling, and all those old-fashioned entertainments involving physical movement. Remember, according to research, time spent boosting happiness pays you back tenfold in rates of overall success.

Of course, studying, which involves very little physical movement, also contributes to happiness as long as it constitutes work done towards a meaningful goal. When students perceive no meaning to their work and feel unable to pursue their true interests, then schoolwork becomes a chore. But as we all know, and as parents remind their children time and time again, sometimes we have to do unpleasant chores in life if we want to achieve long-term goals. Luckily, the above happiness-generating techniques can help students successfully get through school, work, and much of life's general drudgery by keeping happiness levels high, in spite of it all.

The happiness studies that revealed all this information have been an important part of the development of the science of neuroplasticity. Our new understanding that the brain can physically change based upon people consciously changing how they think about things really alters how people have, for years, thought about learning and the brain. For instance, studies show that London cab drivers have enlarged hippocampi (a part of the brain that deals with spacial intelligence) because of all the practice they put into getting around the maze-like city. In another study, monkeys faced with a difficult challenge mastered it, and in so doing expanded the relevant area of their brains. Studies on meditators[24] showed that after just eight weeks of following a daily meditation regimen, the subjects increased the density of their gray matter in structures associated with introspection and compassion while decreasing the density of gray matter in the amygdala—an area associated with anxiety and stress.

In the same way that meditators can increase their gray matter density and cab drivers can expand their hippocampi, if you and your family make a concerted effort to become happier people, your brains will physically change, making everyone more likely to succeed. So as you and your children choose recreational activities, schools, work places, and extracurriculars, it would do you good to base your choices upon the presence or absence of elements proven to increase happiness, such as meaningful goals, opportunities to improve, optimism, relationships, and small rewards.

In designing BrainMatterZ, I kept happiness research in mind. After all, having been a student myself for so many years, I know from first-hand experience that the professors who motivated me to learn, and made me feel good about my potential, produced the best results. Armed with proven scientific support for the fact that happiness leads to success, I designed my BrainMatterZ program around findings such as the three-to-one ratio, the need to utilize a signature strength, the importance of social relationships, and the mood-building effects of exercise, among other findings. Now I can confidently state that BrainMatterZ is an ultra-positive program that uses encouragement paired with honest assessments to build not just cognitive skills, but student self-efficacy and happiness. And we now have empirical evidence that it works.

In the summer of 2018, researchers from the University of Nevada, Reno, conducted a study at the Hollister Elementary School in Hollister, California. Forty-seven students, aged 8 to 12 were divided into two groups. The control group was assessed for visual processing speed using the Wechsler Intelligence Scale for Children (WISC) V assessment tool. The assessment was performed by an independent psychologist. During the study period, the students attended school as usual, with no intervention. The study group was given the same assessment tool by the same independent psychologist. They then received twenty hours of brain training in the BrainMatterZ program which I administered after normal school hours over the course of five weeks. At the conclusion of the study period, both groups were again assessed using the WISC V tool. The study group showed a significant mean improvement over the control group, validating the anecdotal evidence I have been collecting from parents and children over the past ten years. BrainMatterZ works.

The main tool I use to achieve such dramatic results is my own physical presence. As I work with students, I cheerlead, I encourage, I explain, and I affirm. In short, I am not a computer. Cognitive skills-building computer programs have their place, but happiness research has shown incontrovertibly that when students interact with real teachers who believe in them, encourage them, and guide them toward success, their happiness shoots up. Computerized programs do not provide social interaction, nor do they help students identify and utilize signature strengths. Computers can't motivate students to exercise on a balance board, nor can they push students to recover from a mistake, go one step further, and ultimately complete a difficult task. Computers can't offer the warm handshakes, hugs, and small rewards that a personal cognitive-skills coach provides at each session.

As my clients move through the customized cognitive skills drills in BrainMatterZ, I make it clear that I am available to answer any and all questions students may have, which is an important aspect of working one on one. Some of the drills can be quite difficult, and students often ask, "Why do I have to do this?" I confidently and thoroughly answer that question so that students go from being skeptical and hesitant to excited and self-motivated to succeed. By asking such questions, students come to understand that not only will these drills help them succeed in school, but that they will also make them smarter and more quick-witted in general. In short, both my encouragement and my honest discussion of the findings of neuroplasticity motivate students to do their drills, meanwhile building students' interest in the workings of their own brains. This adds to the self-motivated, meaningful aspect of the work that we do.

More than any of the other happiness-study findings, I think the realization that people should find their work to be truly meaningful stands out as a crucial point. As students grow up and choose colleges, then careers, all parents hope they select pursuits that will not only generate financial success but also make them intrinsically happy. In fact, most parents could have told these happiness researchers long ago exactly what their findings would be. After all, we instinctively know that building happiness leads to good things. On a more practical level, we also want our children to succeed. Sometimes it seems like these two desires stand at cross-purposes, but now that science has proven happiness to be a precursor to success, parents can relax and follow their instincts. Informed parents today guide their children toward both the intrinsic rewards of happiness and the extrinsic accomplishments of academics. When these can be accomplished simultaneously, success is a slam dunk!

CHAPTER 6

MAKING THE CUT

The "Grit" Factor

Don't be afraid to give up the good to go for the great!

STEVE PREFONTAINE

Most high-achieving children who work through the BrainMat-terZ program have one goal in mind: admission to the college of their choice. What many students don't realize, though, is that admission to college is just the beginning. Following through and getting that college degree will require students to perform in ways in which they have not yet been tested. In fact, a surprising number of students admitted to college never do complete their degrees. The United States actually leads first-world countries in the number of college dropouts. Scientists have studied this phenomenon in depth and come up with some very interesting conclusions regarding which students finish college and which do not.

Research shows that some of the students with the highest IQs and SAT test scores are the most likely to drop out of college. Ouch! Surprisingly, further research reveals that the answer to having staying-power in college is neither intelligence nor achievement. Instead, success relies upon a few unique personality traits. In one study, the students most likely to succeed in college were those with high scores on something called the

Grit Scale. In another study, a Strength of Character[25] test turned out to be three times more apt to predict college success than any combination of cognitive ratings, SAT scores, or class rank.

The Grit Scale, as developed by researcher Angela Duckworth, very simply asks individuals to rate themselves from one to five on twelve different personality traits that pertain to resilience in the face of obstacles, determination toward long-term goals, and passion for achieving those goals. Researchers followed different test subjects through a variety of difficult situations, including attending college, competing in a national spelling bee, and basic training at West Point military academy. In each and every case, the subjects' individual Grit scores corresponded more highly with success than any other factor, including IQ or standardized test scores.[26] In the Strength of Character study, researchers asked peers to rate one another as to characteristics including conscientiousness, responsibility, being orderly, not being prone to daydreaming, determination, and likeliness to persevere. In both cases—whether subjects rated themselves or were rated by others—character scores tended to directly correspond with success rates, whereas test scores measuring intelligence and achievement showed no correlation.

Researchers also found that high school GPAs corresponded well to high character scores. Surprisingly, this relationship applied across the board, no matter what type or level high school the subject attended. Furthermore, researchers found the relationship between Grit /Strength of Character and high school GPAs to be causative, meaning those with high resilience, self-control, and similar character traits tend to succeed in both high school and college. Amazingly, the research showed (for all but the most challenging universities) that neither intelligence nor acquired knowledge have any perceivable relationship to the likelihood of students graduating from college.

Studies went on to reveal the following list of character traits most likely to lead a college student to the successful completion of a degree:

- Grit
- Self-control
- Zest
- Social intelligence
- Gratitude
- Optimism

These types of studies fascinate me. After all, I developed BrainMatterZ to help parents help their high-achieving students fulfill their dreams and go on to become the world-changing visionaries they hope to be. So—seeing the importance of high school GPA to a student's future, and being, as I am, in the cognitive skills game—I had to wonder about the correlation of cognitive skills to high school GPA. It turns out, in a study of high school seniors, that cognitive scores and a "personality index" are equally predictive of high school GPA.[28] Therefore, it is possible, and indeed logical, to assume that high cognitive skills levels help students develop the personality traits that ensure their graduation from college.

As mentioned in the previous chapter, these ideal personality traits are also proven to contribute to peoples' health and happiness. For instance, self-control, one of the most important personality traits required for success, was the subject of a New Zealand study that showed those who have high levels of it tend not only to be more successful in college, but healthier and happier overall. Children who rated low in self-control tended to be up to three times more likely as adults to smoke, to have health problems, to have bad credit ratings, and to be in trouble with the law than those with high self-control.[29] However, extremely high self-control scores can also lead to lower happiness, as issues such as obsessive-compulsive disorder and unwillingness to take risks come into play. So scientists agree that self-control alone, though statistically important, is not the ideal trait to measure likelihood of success. Out of all the above-listed characteristics, many scientists have chosen to focus on grit as the defining factor for student success. Logically, scientists next asked how we can help students develop grit (which includes self-control as a sub-factor) to a healthy degree.

Research, as mentioned above, has revealed that talent and intelligence are unrelated to success, but there is more. In fact, sometimes talent can be inversely related to success.[30] That means the smartest kids are sometimes the least likely to succeed. It makes a certain amount of sense: if success has come easy to these children all their lives, they simply did not build up the stamina (one of the factors in "grit") during those crucial childhood years for getting through hard times. If a child can solve an equation in ten minutes when other children require an hour, if a child can master dribbling a basketball in a single day when other players require an entire season, if a child has naturally perfect pitch and can sing on key without even trying, that child simply gets used to success coming easy. But let's face it: everyone, at some point, comes upon hard times, be they emotional, financial, physical, or even spiritual. And when naturally talented children eventually do have to face problems they don't know how to solve, they find themselves at a serious disadvantage. Children without natural talents learn to work hard for success early in life. Those with natural talent simply may not have to, and, while one can develop grit at any point in life, not acquiring that personality trait early on can really handicap a child.

However, studies show children who experience hardship early in life do not necessarily develop grit either. Sometimes their hardship leads to a mindset of "learned helplessness,"[31] where they come to believe that no matter what they do, they can't improve themselves, their lives, or the world around them. So while a certain amount of hardship can help children develop grit, it can also have the opposite effect, especially if the hardship is severe. As it turns out, the key to helping children develop grit is not in subjecting them to some carefully prescribed level of hardship, but in teaching them how to think about the hardships they already encounter.

Researcher Carol Dweck studied the grit phenomenon in depth and came up with some very interesting conclusions that teach us how we can actually, and quite easily, instill grit in our children, no matter how much natural talent they may possess. Don't worry, it doesn't involve handicapping the child or disguising his or her natural talents. Instead, it requires yet another paradigm shift—this time, in how we talk about intelligence and how we praise our children. Through numerous studies, Dweck discovered that students who understand that intelligence is not fixed tend to work harder. She calls their way of thinking "growth mindset." These students realize that hard work really will pay off, not just in terms of grades, but also in terms of building their intelligence over the long run.

Students who learn about neuroplasticity and their brain's ability to grow and change also tend to choose more challenging tasks. They confront their failures by devising strategies for future improvement and instead of giving up on challenges, welcome them. Also, they tend to be honest about their grades and achievements, admitting when there is room for improvement and striving to accomplish more. These students tend to develop more emotional resiliency than others, which also results in increased baseline levels of happiness.

By contrast, students who believe intelligence is fixed, or who have a fixed mindset, tend to view academic challenges as tests of their brainpower instead of as opportunities to improve it. These students believe that if a task requires significant effort, it means they aren't smart enough to do it. They subscribe to the notion that, for truly smart kids, no effort would be required. Consequently, these students tend to choose challenges they know they can achieve and avoid things that are likely to be difficult or challenging. Fixed-mindset students tend to focus on looking good academically, in order to prove their innate intelligence, rather than trying hard to build their intelligence. Studies show they also tend to blame others when things don't go their way and avoid challenges that might may make them look bad.

For these students, interest in learning is low, even among those who know they have high IQs. They tend not to recover from setbacks well and also tend more toward cheating and lying about their grades. When they succeed, these students often acquire a false sense of superiority undermined by deep self-doubt. The fixed-mindset students tend to feel the need to prove themselves again and again, causing anxiety, insecurity, and general unhappiness.

To understand just how these findings were made, let's take one example of Dweck's many experiments. It concerns two groups of low-achieving students about to enter the seventh grade. In a course preparing them for the rigors of the year ahead, teachers instructed them in study, time-management, and memorizing skills. One group also learned the latest findings in neuroplasticity, regarding how the brain grows and develops based upon its experiences. Even though both groups of students learned the strategies needed to improve their math scores, only the group primed to have a growth mindset actually did improve its grades.[32]

Interestingly, when Alfred Binet developed the IQ test, he never meant for it to be a test of fixed intelligence. He always viewed it as a baseline measurement designed to determine which students needed extra help in order to improve. Unfortunately, the test has long been used by many school districts to determine a student's intellectual potential, partly because, until recently, scientists did not know how to build intelligence. But with science's new understanding of cognitive skills, we now have that knowledge and can return to Binet's original intention for the use of IQ tests. More importantly, we can inform students of these findings and integrate the knowledge into how we talk about their accomplishments.

In her research, Dweck discovered that when students are praised for their intelligence, rather than for hard work or persistence, they tend to develop a fixed mindset. This means they receive a short burst of pride followed by a fear of falling behind or disappointing those who praised them. Meanwhile, students who receive praise for their hard work, persistence, strategizing, engagement, perseverance, and improvement tend to develop a growth mindset. They understand that success depends upon developing certain winning personality traits and, as a result, they truly have no limits on how far they can reach.

For instance, the following types of praise tend to build a growth mindset and grit:

- "Excellent work! When your first attempt didn't succeed, you tried again and again until you found a way that worked. I like that way of thinking. Nothing can stop you!"
- "Do you see the improvement from the last test to this one? You must have worked hard and put in a lot of study hours. That's what I like to see. You never give up!"
- "I saw how hard you worked on that science project. The results really show that you concentrated and made this assignment a priority. That's exactly what it takes to win the science fair."

By contrast, the following types of praise tend to build a fixed mindset, which in the long run actually reduces student motivation and love of learning:

- "Wow, you got an A! That's my boy, the smartest one in the class. You are really going to go far with a brilliant mind like yours."
- "What a wonderful report card. I can always count on you to make me proud. I must have done something right to have such smart kids!"
- "Congratulations on winning the science fair! It shows you are the smartest student in your class, just as I always thought."

Surprising, isn't it? Without this explanation of growth versus fixed mindsets, most people wouldn't even notice the difference between these two types of praise. Parents have always known praising their children is important—and certainly any praise is better than no praise at all—but now that studies have shown praise type alone is a primary factor for determining student mindsets, it makes sense to learn how to properly praise in order to build the all-important grit your children need for success.

Incidentally, the findings of neuroplasticity apply not just to intelligence, but also to creativity, athletics, artistic ability, and, of course, personality traits. Just as any child or adult has the ability to become smarter, he or she also has the ability to develop grit, gain athletic skill, learn to draw, or play a musical instrument. It is important, however, not to let the growth mindset work against itself. Some high-performing children may take their knowledge of neuroplasticity to the point where they feel pressure to improve in more areas than they really have time or energy to pursue, just because they know the brain is capable of doing so.

In offering praise, remind your children that you know their success is the result of working both harder and smarter and that when it comes to the work we do, we must all consciously choose the things we spend our time on. Smart time-management choices should result in improvement in those areas students judge to be most important. After all, no matter how much energy your child has, he or she must make choices as to where to expend that energy. This is one reason why improving cognitive skills pays off so well. No matter what choice your child ultimately makes in terms of career, hobbies, and extracurriculars, improving cognitive skills across the board will help with each and every one of those pursuits.

It's interesting for me to look at all this research and think back to my days coaching basketball. In sports, the notion of fixed mindset and growth mindset comes into play, just as it does in academics. I have certainly encountered those players who possess natural ability, and I know such skill can be a double-edged sword. Such players are often unwilling to try plays that might challenge them. They want to simply shoot basket after basket and complain about participating in drills, teamwork, assists, and other aspects of training necessary for any well-rounded player. Coaches have always known that in order to work with these players, we must insist that they participate in the same hard work and fundamentals drills as the other players. After all, while every team needs a good shooter, no team can function if everyone specializes. So, once again, it comes down to having every player master a broad range of fundamental skills.

Dweck's research on praise particularly interests me, as her findings are something I think coaches have known—but probably wouldn't have been able to explain so eloquently—for centuries. Whether before a game, during a huddle, or in a postgame wrap-up, we instinctively praise effort instead of natural ability. Any sports team that is led to believe it can coast on natural ability is bound for certain and speedy disappointment. Perhaps because, in sports, competition is everything, the inherent need to develop grit is never hidden.

Competition certainly comes into play in academics as well, but perhaps in a less obvious way. When parents encourage students before a science test, they don't usually say, "Crush those other students! Destroy them!" And rightly so. Whether people have fixed or growth mindsets, they understand that academic work is a competition against oneself, a constant effort to improve one's own skills. Perhaps this difference explains a bit about why it has taken so long for the growth-mindset principle, which has long been a staple of sports coaching, to reach the realm of academia.

In any case, I'm glad researchers have finally pinpointed the important elements of appropriate praise and teaching neuroplasticity as essential to the effort to instill grit in students. I have, of course, made those elements essential aspects of the BrainMatterZ program, so, once again, parents who provide this type of coaching for their children can rest assured that, as an educational psychologist, I am not lax with my language. The instructions I give, the praise I dole out, and the type of encouragement I provide my clients is all directly based upon neuroscientific research. As BrainMatterZ expands, I will train additional educational psychologists to work as I do. My intent is not only to teach them these principles, but to ensure that my sisters and brothers in psychology are as fascinated by this subject matter as I am. Neuroplasticity research, of course, continues, and as each new finding appears, I want to ensure that my team capitalizes upon its benefits.

Along with building cognitive skills, developing both happiness and grit are essential to helping your children succeed. Interestingly, instilling happiness and grit in our children has more to do with how we view things, talk about things, and interpret life's events than it does with any type of schoolwork. Sometimes, I think in their efforts to offer their children the best education available—private schooling, test-prep classes, online education, learning toys, tutors, and so forth—many parents miss the fact that the very best way we can help children is simply by encouraging them to think in an education-positive and self-positive way. Part and parcel of this way of thinking is taking a coach's attitude of guiding students in the development of their educational game plan, just as a basketball coach helps each team develop a unique, winning game plan.

Sure, sometimes we have to learn how exactly to do this. We didn't all come from such forward-thinking backgrounds, and even if we did, scientific advances now present us with more information on establishing a growth mindset than our parents ever had access to. It just goes to show that when parents educate themselves about how to promote things like cognitive skills and happiness and grit, and how to place their children in that type of positive-thinking environment, that knowledge base alone actually turns out to be the best gift they can give their children.

CHAPTER 7

THE X's AND O's OF LEARNING

Rules of the Brain Game

Excellence is not a singular act, but a habit.
You are what you repeatedly do.

SHAQUILLE O'NEAL

Part of my mission in writing this book is to bridge the ongoing disconnect between neuroscience and education. Advances in our understanding of neuroplasticity are being made every day, and in order to build the education system that this country, this world, and your child deserve, that information must be brought into schools. Yet teachers already have their hands full developing and implementing curricula, and administrators are up to their eyeballs ensuring the efficiency of school staff, systems, and buildings. Surely, every school should appoint a scientist whose sole job is to keep educators on the cutting edge of neuroscientific research, but somehow that hasn't happened ... yet. In fact—given the newfound importance of everyday issues such as the type of praise a parent gives a child—neuroplasticity information needs a conduit for becoming common knowledge in family homes, too. This is where the role of an educational psychologist comes into play.

The country's most advanced private schools do employ professionals such as myself, and in that capacity I am able to fulfill the role of both psychologist and neuroscience researcher-in-residence. When I worked at Cate School, I saw the students I worked with improve by leaps and bounds; however, even at Cate I didn't see students until they experienced a learning or emotional concern of some kind. Solving problems is a big part of what I do, but I feel that educating students about how their brains work and how best to approach learning so as to thrive helps more. Such an inclusive, overall approach to educational psychology blankets a learning environment with right-thinking approaches that enable students to solve their own problems more readily.

Your home is a learning environment, too, and I feel that if parents utilize neuroscientific advances in everyday life, this will enable them to break certain cycles of tradition in education and child-rearing that have simply been proven not to be best-practice. After all, intimidating children into working hard with threats of corporal punishment used to be considered a perfectly reasonable strategy for getting results. Public humiliation, such as the dunce cap or making errant children stand in a corner, is now considered laughably archaic. Such strategies originally developed out of teacher and administrator ignorance as to how children learn and what truly motivates them. Now we know better, and yet, even today, many important facts about the learning process are still not generally known or utilized, resulting in learning systems that continue to employ inefficient and archaic methods.

A more thorough background in brain science will simply help students and parents make better educational decisions. In fact, with all of today's technology at our fingertips, neuroscientific information should be keeping the cultures of all first-world nations on the cutting edge of educational psychology. To match our plastic brains we need a plastic educational culture, which changes and grows with each new finding. With this in mind, let's discuss some more findings of recent neuroscientific research. Some of them are rather intuitive, and others might surprise you, but when scientifically backed they provide a bit of extra impetus for us to work this information into our lifestyles and learning or teaching experiences.

PHYSICAL FITNESS DRIVES BRAIN FITNESS

The first rule of thumb, when it comes to keeping the brain active, applies whether one is trying to prepare for a standardized test or to prevent the onset of dementia. Human beings evolved to move (to hunt, to gather, to lift, to build, to walk, to run), and the brain improves when the body exercises. Even though the brain itself is an organ, not a muscle, the increased blood flow and endorphin production provided by exercise benefits the brain while also building muscle. In fact, research has proven that one of the most important factors in preventing senility is not a tendency to read great works or the ability to play chess, but the fact of having a physically active lifestyle. More specifically, science has shown that regular exercise increases long-term memory, reason, attention, problem-solving, and fluid intelligence—all aspects of the ability to reason quickly and think abstractly while utilizing learned knowledge. Exercise has not been shown to improve short-term memory; however. it does lower your odds of getting Alzheimer's, a disease related to short-term memory, by more than 60 percent.[33] Exercise is not a magic bullet or an ultimate prescription for neuropsychological perfection, but it provides a significant, proven, lifelong advantage for brain health.[34]

In addition to offering long-term benefits, studies show exercise provides a short-term brain boost as well. When children jogged for thirty minutes, two to three times per week, for twelve weeks, they showed significantly improved cognitive performance.[35] When they stopped doing so, their cognitive scores returned to pre-exercise levels. Another study showed that physically fit children identify visual stimuli much faster than sedentary ones,[36] and still another study demonstrated that physically fit children and adolescents allocate more cognitive resources to a task, and for longer periods of time, than couch-potato kids.[37]

Further studies show that, for adults, even brief walks, when added to the regimen of a non-exerciser, provide significant benefit , although aerobic and strength-building exercises—for thirty minutes, two to three times per week—provide a much higher level of cognitive benefit. But, just like with anything generally beneficial, one can also go too far. The brain needs rest, too, and excessive exercise and exhaustion can hurt your thinking power. After all, you wouldn't ask someone who had just finished a marathon to try to solve a trigonometry equation. In order to keep the brain at peak performance, students should integrate an adequate balance of rest and exercise into their lifestyles.

Finally, one of the most important ways that exercise affects the brain is in preventing depression. Exercise literally regulates the release of dopamine, serotonin, and norepinephrine: neurotransmitters associated with mental health. Everyone on the planet prefers to lead a happy life, but now that we know happiness itself leads to success, not the other way around, the importance of regular exercise for students of all ages really stands out.

ATTENTION IS THE SECRET SAUCE

In order to learn, we first must pay attention. Scientists have studied the phenomenon of attention in an effort to determine exactly what makes people focus and what causes minds to wander. In so doing, they actually have isolated two different types of attention, or alertness. The first is called intrinsic alertness and describes peoples' normal levels of paying attention to the world around them. The second is called phasic alertness, which describes our reactions to something surprising, alarming, or novel. Once the phasic alert system is employed, perhaps by a perceived emergency, exciting situation, or wonderful opportunity, the brain engages its executive function skills in order to decide how to react to the stimulus. Run for cover? Fight an intruder? Laugh and smile? Help a friend? As part of this research, scientists were actually able to identify four elements of any situation that engage the phasic alert system: emotions, meaning, focus, and timing.[38]

People react to and remember emotionally triggering events much more than neutral ones. Most likely you didn't need a scientist to tell you that. What you may not have known is the fact that in remembering an emotional event, we tend to recall the overall gist, or meaning, of the event while we often get the details wrong. Science has further shown that when we remember the big picture and its intrinsic meaning to us, we can then reapply our intelligence to memorizing related factual details, but this must be done with deliberate effort. So in order to keep our interest, a situation must grab our attention with emotional impact. Then we will react by understanding the overall meaning of the event, after which, if we chose to, we can make a deliberate attempt to attach the details of the event to that larger, meaning-based memory. In short, emotion drives attention, and attention drives memory.

Another aspect of attention is a fact you may find disturbing: the brain cannot multitask. Or, as scientists put it: "The brain is biologically incapable of processing attention-rich inputs simultaneously.[39]" This means that when we pay attention to many things at once, our working memory is actually functioning with a switchboard-like mechanism that enables us to focus on one thing after another in a continuous cycle. Those with better working memories will be able to switch tasks with more speed and frequency; however, learning is always improved by eliminating this extra stressor. Attention works best on one thing at a time.

Finally, timing is crucial to retaining student attention. Here is another example of an instance where neuroscientific research should be directly applied to every classroom, though it rarely is. Student attention to any given lecture subject tends to fade after a ten-minute period, so a wise teacher would plan lectures to begin with a brief, one-minute explanation of a general idea, including an emotionally charged meaning. If the teacher followed this with nine minutes of details attached to that larger meaning, students' minds would be more likely to connect those dots.[40]

If each ten-minute period of a class were planned like this, and if each meaning invoked an emotional response from students, teachers would thus utilize the rules of attention to take best advantage of the brain's natural processes.

When teaching in cycles like this, one more aspect of learning comes into play. At each ten-minute point, the student's brain literally needs a rest from learning, even if the rest period only lasts for a few seconds. The brain learns best in spaced repetition cycles, where the mind can rest in-between. A mere joke or anecdote can supply the much-needed feeling of rest and relaxation. Even if a teacher briefly changes the subject to what's being served in the cafeteria that day, it can help provide the short break students' brains require to reapply attention to the next ten-minute learning cycle. This idea certainly sounds like a major overhaul of today's typical class lecture system, but with some time for adjustment, both teachers and students could find spaced-repetition lectures easier both to give and to receive.

THE SENSES FEED THE MIND

Cognitive psychologists have proven that learning improves when information is provided via more than one sense. This means that a lecture including both an auditory portion and a pictorial presentation will sink in deeper than either one of those components alone. Students taught with such multi-sensory approaches have more accurate and longer-lasting recall than others—not just by a little, but by 50 to 75 percent! Also, when the element of touch is added to a multi-sensory approach, students tend to recall information up to 30 percent better than without it. The core of this discovery lies in the fact that the more information given at the moment of learning, the better the ability to recall. This is like asking the brain to rub its belly and pat its head at once: the extra work required to take in all that additional input turbo-charges the brain, causing it to take the input deeper into the memory than usual. The phenomenon of multi-sensory learning actually speeds up response time, increases accurate recall, and enriches encoding at the moment of learning, because sensory processes in the brain are wired to work together.

Those who wish to benefit from learning through the senses should keep in mind that not only do students learn better from words and pictures than from words alone, but that they learn better when the words and pictures are presented simultaneously, not successively. Also, research has shown that when utilizing textbooks students benefit most from corresponding words and pictures being presented nearby each other, rather than on different areas of a page. Furthermore, the less extraneous information cluttering the focus of the lecture, the better. Teachers should keep in mind also that narration appeals to the auditory sense, while written text is a visual phenomenon, so audio narration, rather than written text, should accompany a pictorial or animated presentation. The element of kinesthetics comes into play as well. Students who act out their lessons or otherwise integrate physical movement into learning tend to benefit even more than those who simply watch and listen.

The sense of smell can also promote massive information recall, especially when paired with strong emotional stimuli. For instance, an emotional experience associated with smell will be recalled when the subject re-experiences the smell. In fact, anything learned in the presence of a particular smell will be better recalled when that smell is present. It is a bit more difficult to integrate the sense of smell into classroom learning, as one can't guarantee the reappearance of any particular scent during test-taking; regardless, the more senses utilized to teach any particular point, the better.[41]

STRESS ABOUT SUCCESS

Research has shown that the human stress response is well designed to deal with immediate emergency situation, but badly designed for long-term stress-filled lifestyles, a fact that doesn't bode well for students in high-pressure situations. Our organs, hormones, and bodily systems are designed for primitive survival.

When confronted by stress, they increase physical and mental power just over the amount of time it takes to escape an attack, and no longer. Furthermore, the body and brain require time to rest and rejuvenate after each stressful moment, and when they don't get this, the system breaks down: the body becomes ill, and the brain stops thinking clearly. However, a situation one person perceives as stressful might seem like pure fun to another, so before talking about the damage caused by stress, let's look at what exactly stress is.

According to researchers Jeansok Kim and David Diamond, a stressor must produce "an aroused physiological response" that is measurable by an outside party.[42] For instance, if a child is afraid of dogs and cries whenever he sees one, that crying fulfills the requirement of a physiological response labeling dogs as stressors for that child. By the same token, if students are so stressed by tests that their palms sweat and breathing becomes shallow, those tests can be considered stressors.

Secondly, the subject must consider the stressor to be aversive. After all, people enjoy many things that produce physiological responses, such as roller coasters, stage performances, and surprise parties, so the issue of the stressor being aversive is entirely determined by the individual.

Third, the subject must feel out of control when faced with the stressor. The frightened child faced with the dog, for instance, feels he cannot defend himself, and stressed students preparing for tests feel unable to master the material. Here again we encounter the issue of a fixed or growth mindset. Students who believe intelligence is fixed think they truly can't improve their skills or knowledge in the subject area and therefore feel out of control; whereas students with a growth mindset experience less stress around the test because they know they can improve both their knowledge of the subject matter and the cognitive skills required to master the test.

When stress—a physiological response to an aversive stimulus that makes the subject feel out of control—presents itself, the body releases adrenaline and cortisol, which enable one to either run away, fight for survival, or quickly think of a clever solution to the problem. Scientists suggest this system developed evolutionarily during the time when peoples' primary stressors were wild animal attacks. Typically such attacks (whether the person survived or not) would not last long. But today, especially for children and teens, stressors tend to take the form of ongoing relationship problems, high workloads, and competition for high honors. These long-term stressors don't allow the body's emergency protocol system to function as designed: acting, then resting, then acting again. Instead, they require the human brain to exist in what amounts to a constant state of emergency, where stress hormones endlessly recirculate through the body, causing a great deal of physiological harm. Research shows people under stress are unable to concentrate; are less creative; do not perform well on math or language tests; have poor short- and long-term memories; and fail to adapt learned knowledge for new problem-solving situations. Stress also hurts executive function, one of the brain's crucial cognitive skills.[43] Worst of all, chronic stress, and the hormonal imbalance that tends to accompany it, causes depression.

Students tend to be stressed by the following combination of realities: they feel that a great deal is being asked of them, and they have no control over how well they will perform. When we speak of high-achieving, visionary students, the pressure often comes from within. These students want a lot out of life and push themselves to achieve it. In these cases, the best way we can help them avoid stress is by ensuring they do feel in control of their performance. When we educate students about their cognitive skills and their plastic IQs, while also developing those cognitive skills, we reduce their stress levels. We further reduce stress by showing them how we can test their cognitive skills levels, and then by improving them. Giving students this sense of power over their intellects, test results, and overall lives reduces depression, increases happiness, and makes students more likely to succeed. In this manner, cognitive skills training works on so many more levels than just the mechanical effect of the training itself.

VISION RULES THE SENSES

When it comes to remembering something, visual input takes precedence over written or spoken input, but this information is not new. Scientists have known for more than one hundred years that visual input is more quickly and accurately recalled by the brain than any other input. As you take that in, understand that words, in this case, are not considered visual input. The brain does view words as pictures, but each word is a symbol, which represents something other than itself, and must be decoded, whereas a picture looks exactly (or somewhat) like what it is. The process of mentally decoding word-pictures into real-looking mental pictures is complex and slows down processing. So when we talk about visual input, in this case we mean actual pictures.

Research shows students remember information that is only presented orally at a rate of 10 percent, as compared to 65 percent memory recall when a picture is added to the presentation. As discussed earlier, a multi-sensory approach to learning is best because it forces the brain to work harder to take in all that input, thus opening the student up to a peak state of learning. Smell, touch, hearing, and kinesthetics all come into play when we talk about multi-sensory education; however, vision dominates them all. Studies show humans rely upon vision partially because, as babies, we develop the ability to use visual cues quite early.

Babies understand that objects appearing together tend to be part of a larger object, like spots on a leopard. They also understand perspective, in that they realize an object growing larger is actually coming closer. In both babies and adults, the brain's visual cortex stands out as being far larger than areas used for perception of other senses. When we consider how long it takes a baby to learn language, as compared to how long it takes to learn to see, it becomes clear that vision is our most well-practiced and most useful sensory-learning tool. In fact, 90 percent of information that comes to the brain is visual.[44]

Leaders in business and education have attempted to take advantage of the brain's hunger for visual input by developing presentation programs such as PowerPoint. These could be incredibly useful to the learning process but usually are not utilized correctly. After all, most PowerPoint presentations feature bullet points on a screen. A few pictures are often thrown in for decoration, but here, once again, we encounter words in both audio and visual format. To take advantage of the brain's love of visual input, such presentations should focus on pictures directly related to the words being orally spoken and stay away from the non-pictorial, symbolic use of the written word.[45] The more research scientists conduct on neuroplasticity, the better we, as a community, can help visionary children excel. Sometimes all it takes is small changes to our lifestyles and language. Children who push themselves for intellectual stimulation, or who respond to stressors by striving to be the great problem-solvers of tomorrow, encounter unique problems. They often do not realize how to go about achieving their ambitious goals in a logical, efficient manner. Teaching students about neuroplasticity and their own cognitive skills is, of course, crucial to helping them move forward without wasted effort or undue stress. Additionally, we can help them by ensuring that their lessons include multi-sensory, especially visual, input, and that lessons are timed according to the brain's natural attention span. And, let's not forget, including regular exercise into family and school culture activates the brains of students and parents alike, leading to happier, healthier, and more productive families.

I developed BrainMatterZ as a path toward ideal, neuroscientifically supported education aimed at helping ambitious students get where they want to go as efficiently and stress-free as possible. The exercises, timing, and multi-sensory approaches built into the BrainMatterZ system aim to make a single hour of study into a week's worth of benefit. But the advantages don't have to end at my doorstep. Each and every one of the scientific revelations in this chapter can be employed at home, at school, and even in your workplace, to get more productivity and happiness out of each and every day.

CHAPTER 8

TEST ANXIETY

Choking at the Academic Free-Throw Line

I am not anxious. I am just extremely well-educated about all the things that can go catastrophically wrong!

UNKNOWN

Test anxiety looms as one of the biggest academic obstacles for students of all ages. In fact, studies show that as people's motivation to succeed increases, their likelihood of failing does, too.[46] When it comes to standardized tests, as well as other academic exams, it seems like sometimes the best students achieve the worst scores. Science has proven this to be true: more experience in an academic area can often lead to worse performance in a testing environment, not better.[47] In studying this phenomenon, researchers have found it occurs because the brain has two types of memory, but only one can be consciously accessed.

When people memorize detailed instructions for tasks that eventually become commonplace—such as how to tie a shoe—the details end up stored in something called procedural memory, in the subconscious. After we have tied our one-thousandth shoe, we don't need to consciously think about the details anymore. This certainly makes sense, as we could never learn anything new if we had to continue concentrating on each and every daily task we learned from preschool on up. However, for a child just learning to tie a shoe, the details of the activity still reside in what researchers call the explicit memory, which is part of the conscious mind.

Now, think for a moment what would happen if you had to quickly list each and every step in the process of tying a shoe. If you could even do it, this would take some time. You would have to envision the shoe, or perhaps even reach down to your shoe and actually tie it, writing down the step-by-step instructions as you re-experience them. But if we asked a preschool child to tell us how to tie a shoe, the little imp would probably rattle off the most incredibly detailed list of instructions you ever heard, including variations for extra security, speed, and flair. Along those lines, remember the old expression: "It's like riding a bike!" Of course, this means that once you learn you never forget how to ride a bike. But the truth is, once you learn to do it, the skill goes into procedural memory, and your conscious mind absolutely does forget how to do it. You will never fail to ride a bike again, but you probably will fail any test on the step-by-step instructions for bicycling.

Because of this tendency for learned knowledge to become unconscious, students with less experience—or with more of the relevant knowledge still residing in their explicit memories—often outperform more knowledgeable students on tests. One simple solution to this problem is to have higher-level students study with lower-level students during test-prep time (or anytime, actually). Such arrangements seem, on the surface, to benefit the less-experienced students, and they do, but they may benefit the experienced students even more, as helping teach and tutor will force procedural knowledge back up to the explicit, conscious memories.[48]

WHEN NOT TO THINK

Interestingly, when a test requires one simply to do a learned task without any explanation or analysis, students who fail to perform tend to do so for the opposite reason: they overthink it.

Nervousness causes everyone from students to athletes to obsess upon the work at hand, thus bringing procedural knowledge, which functions best without any conscious thought at all, up to the explicit level, where one loses the natural flow of the activity. For instance, if I asked you to tie your shoe right now, you would do it expertly in an instant, but if I asked you to explain what you were doing as you tied it, your words and movements would become more awkward and hesitant.

This is the type of problem experienced by Olympic athletes who have performed gold-medal-worthy work before but fail to do so at crunch time. In these cases, research shows that the best way to succeed is to fight the urge to bring that ice-skating routine or ski-jump maneuver up to conscious memory. Instead, when the urge to overthink-it strikes you, sing a little song, instead count backward by threes, or list all the state capitals you know. Distract the brain from the conscious mind's attempt to sabotage information that has, essentially, become instinctual. But this is not the only time when overthinking a problem can be your downfall.

Studies show students with high working memory, which is directly related to IQ, often find it more difficult to think outside the box and to come up with innovative solutions than those with low working memory. In fact, students with ADHD (attention deficit hyperactivity disorder) have been proven superior to non-ADHD students in generating creative and unusual solutions to problems.[49] Some scientists believe this stems from high-working-memory students' inherent ability to inhibit irrelevant information from infecting a memorized problem-solving procedure. The ADHD students, because they are unable to inhibit random information from coming to mind, tend to come up with more unusual solutions. So on certain tests and in certain real-life situations, believe it or not, being "smarter" (or having more working memory) can actually hold students back. This seems like the world's weirdest problem to have. But then again, "I failed the test because I was too smart to pass," is a much better excuse than, "The dog ate my homework."

This discrepancy in ability types is another reason why different types of students should study together. While experienced students can help beginners, artistic students can help scientific ones, athletic students can help the science nerds, and vice versa. When different types of students study and work together, exactly how they are helping each other may not be readily apparent, but the brain takes in these differences in study styles and catalogues them for future use. Just seeing an out-of-the-box thinker at work can provide useful information for more scientifically-oriented students to store away. By the same token, when students attend advanced high schools, which essentially isolate high-working-memory students from the general population, they may confront more test anxiety than they would otherwise—not just because of the competition, but because the culture is so strongly oriented toward utilizing explicit, instead of procedural, memory and inhibiting "irrelevant" problem-solving information.

During the two years that I spent developing BrainMatterZ and working at the prestigious Cate School, I became very aware of these issues coming into play for students who did not test well. Consequently, I oriented part of the program toward helping students understand when a learning or testing environment demands they use procedural versus explicit memory. That means recognizing creative challenges—when step-by-step, problem-solving methods won't work—versus the typical, logical challenges most tests present.

But far more than my advice, improving cognitive skills across the board helps students make these determinations for themselves. Of course, improving working memory scores are always part of the program, but because we also endeavor to improve processing speed, attention, and many more cognitive skills, this work assists students not just with test taking, but also problem solving, planning, and prioritizing.

CALLING A TIME OUT

The same research, much of which was conducted at the Human Performance Lab at the University of Chicago, reveals an even deeper reason why the most high-performing students often underperform on tests, sometimes even to the point of achieving similar test scores to beginners. The issue has to do with the complexity of the given task. Most mental tasks, such as solving complex equations, can be performed extremely accurately with a detailed series of steps, and most high-achieving students, in ordinary life, tend to address complex mental tasks in this manner; whereas, most low-achieving students tend, instead, to use shortcuts, garnering less-accurate results. However, when students feel pressured, especially by a timed test, even the high-achieving students will often switch to the shortcuts, thus reducing the accuracy of results. In fact, the beginners, with their extensive experience utilizing shortcuts, may actually test better than the experts in these cases.

Of course, we all want test scores to reflect each student's true ability (otherwise there would be no point to testing), so researchers have discovered some methods by which high-achieving students can "stay in the zone," as we say in basketball. First of all, panic tends to cause students to choose the shortcut rather than the detailed problem-solving method. To overcome panic, students should learn to pause right in the beginning of a test challenge. Racing ahead is a surefire way to abandon all one has learned and perform exactly like a rookie. Instead, students should take a breath, don't rush, and think about the problem's various solutions, before proceeding—much like an athlete who stops to take a breath before shooting at the free-throw line. By the same token, if the problem is one that requires creativity, flow, physical grace, or improvisation, students need to learn *not* to pause, but to let instinct be their guide. Being able to distinguish between the two types of challenges (such as a violin recital versus a calculus test) will help students tremendously.

In a study comparing how physics professors versus undergraduate physics students solved problems, researchers found that professors were not at all faster at solving the problems. They were, of course, more accurate, because they paused and thought about each problem before attempting to solve it. Some professors even got up from the testing table and took a little walk before attempting to solve a problem. However, once the professors began their problem-solving attempts, they performed faster than the undergraduates. The study proved that letting the mind wander and explore possibilities provides a much-needed incubation period. During this period, the mind isolates relevant problem details from irrelevant ones, thus invoking that "aha" moment for which all great thinkers strive. This method of problem solving does, of course, take more time overall, and we're going to talk about that issue in a moment.

In addition to pausing before attempting to solve a problem, research also shows that test scores improve when subjects take a short break after each problem. Just as muscles become tired after overuse, so does the brain. Concerted effort spent on a difficult reasoning task depletes the brain of glucose, and it will need a moment to recharge its energy supply. If students fail to pause after each test problem, their glucose stores will gradually decrease as the test goes on, making them feel more and more tired and unable to think. That burned-out feeling after a test is due to depleted glucose, but students don't have to feel that way. The brain needs nothing more than regular moments of rest and relaxation to recharge its own energy stores. Especially for those students utilizing complex problem-solving techniques instead of shortcuts (thus depleting their glucose stores more than other students), these breaks are essential to scoring well on tests.

Now, let's talk about how students can get the extra time needed to perform their best. When, as part of the BrainMatterZ program (or any cognitive-skills training program), we give students the full battery of cognitive-skills tests, we discover whether or not they score particularly low in any area. If they do score low, this gives us fair and legal right to apply for additional time on standardized tests. Generally students do receive that time, but the schools and college boards have the final say.

This benefit should not be overlooked or underestimated. Extra test time enables high-achieving students to utilize their complex problem-solving skills in order to get a fair representation on the test results.

Time to prepare before solving a problem, time to rest after solving a problem, and time to consider if the question is one for procedural or explicit memory all benefit a student immeasurably. In particular, if a student suffers from an under-functioning cognitive skill, he or she simply needs that additional time in order to test equally with other students. Cognitive testing has long been a staple of special education programs, enabling those students with known cognitive defects to get the extra time they desperately need. Now, as cognitive skills testing becomes more well-known in high-performing academic circles, school systems can also provide such needed boosts to high-performing students who simply require extra time to access all the brilliance their minds have to offer.

BENEFITS OF SIMULATION

Human Performance Lab research has revealed a great deal more interesting information about how and when people perform at their best. One of these discoveries is so instructive that I worked it in as an essential element of the BrainMatterZ program. Studies show that any simulation of a high-pressure situation will prepare students for facing that situation. Even if the simulation only produces a small fraction of the amount of pressure of the real environment, such practice is shown to significantly raise test scores as compared to students who did not practice in simulated high-pressure situations.[50]

For instance, in one study a group of police officers practiced shooting rubber dummies, who returned fire with fake bullets, while another group practiced shooting only at cardboard targets. Across the board, those who practiced shooting at the rubber dummies returning fire turned out to perform better under real-life, high-stress situations than those who shot at cardboard dummies. Even though they knew they couldn't be hurt by the dummies' fake bullets, the police officers' brains internalized the stress of the return-fire scenario, which conditioned their brains to keep cool under pressure.

Additional studies have shown that the ability to think clearly under pressure is the primary characteristic that separates top-level sports players from lower-level professionals. To achieve that skill, athletes, students, and –business people must simply practice under simulations of the high-pressure situations they anticipate. This is why in the BrainMatterZ program we "make the practice harder than the game." I create a timed testing environment complete with the distractions of music, noise, and talking. In addition, the cognitive skills activities must be completed under the same difficult conditions. Sometimes I literally jump up and down in front of the students as they attempt to perform a timed activity. Invariably, the students laugh at my antics, but they also benefit by finding real standardized tests relaxing in comparison.

This isn't just silliness; it is a scientifically proven method for improving performance. In fact, such simulations would work just as well for business leaders as they do for students, just as well for artists as they do for athletes. I first developed this technique as a coach, when I created similar high-pressure situations for my players during practice. That way, when they had to perform during a real game, they already knew what to expect and how to react. From then to now, it has been my firm belief that both students and athletes need to spend time specially preparing for high-pressure situations in order to deliver their best performance.

THE LIMITS OF SPECIFICITY

Studies on the science of practice actually prove that practice not only improves brain function but also changes the physical wiring of the brain. For instance, when performing tasks related to motor coordination and athletics, professional and amateur soccer players performed similarly; but when the tasks related specifically to the game of soccer, professionals excelled far above the amateurs. This aspect of brain function is called specificity, and it means that, for instance, when students practice doing algebra equations in a classroom environment, they get good at doing algebra *in a classroom environment*, but when they practice doing algebra as part of a timed, standardized test, they get good at *algebra tests*. By the same token, in order to relate algebra to real-life problems, students would have to practice algebra in real-life settings.[51]

Of course, our brains are not so specific that students can't transfer a mathematics skill from one environment to another, but in order to truly excel in one specific environment, such as that of standardized testing (which in no way resembles the complexity of real life or the hectic environment of a classroom), students must actually practice in a simulation of that environment. A basketball player, for instance, can keep up her general athletic skill, coordination, and reflexes by cross-training with soccer, softball, and lacrosse. All those sports require some of the same athletic skills required by basketball, and cross-training is a great way to stay in shape; however, to truly become great at basketball itself, a player must play *basketball itself*, in a court setting, against resistance under pressure. The brain's specificity demands it.

Come to think of it, if a player wants to win on a television reality show, the last thing she should practice is the relevant skill in reality. Instead, she should practice under a mild simulation of the type of stress encountered on the show. For better or worse, competitions, standardized tests, and even reality shows are ways our culture tests people in order to compare them, rank them, and direct them into appropriate channels for their lives and careers. However, these tests are not simulations of reality, so let's face that slightly disturbing fact straight away. Neuroscience supports the assertion that testing doesn't actually test a student's ability to perform a skill, but rather his or her ability to *perform on a test*. For ambitious students, such tests can make or break their college careers, so practicing the skill of testing itself is time well spent.

THE SIDE-EFFECTS OF WORRYING

Research shows that students who worry about their performance on a test tend to score lower. It also shows that those with high working memories do tend to worry more. The same studies show that worrying literally uses the same language-centered part of the brain as test-taking (no matter what the subject of the test), so worrying actually robs the brain of problem-solving energy.[52] Again, this pesky research is telling us that the smarter the student, the worse test results he or she might receive. Let's look on the bright side of this equation: if your children have high working memories and well-functioning cognitive skills, they might be testing lower than their potential. They can achieve better test scores by learning how to sidestep worrying.

Studies show students with low working memories generally tend to make excuses for their failures, such as, "No one in my family is any good at math," while those with high working memories put themselves under more pressure, instead blaming themselves for their failures. Interestingly, the students who make excuses for themselves tend to experience *less* anxiety at test time and sometimes outperform the higher-working-memory students. The theory goes: these students have given themselves permission to fail, so they don't worry; as a result, they don't fail. So mindset makes a big difference when it comes to test performance, and eliminating worry and mental stressors plays a large part in that.

When students experience stress, such as in a testing situation, their cortisol levels tend to go up. What is interesting here is that some students thrive on high cortisol levels while others do not. Math-anxious students experience high-cortisol symptoms—such as sweaty palms, queasy stomachs, and rapid pulses—as indicators that the situation is hopeless, while others interpret the same symptoms as positive signs of an impending, unique challenge. Might it be possible to teach all students to view sweaty palms and a racing heart as signs that the brain is actively engaging and ready to work? Might it be possible to teach students to view self-doubt as the first step in a process of massive self-improvement? Indeed, with effort these things are possible. As such, students should be able to significantly reduce the amount of energy expended toward worry and redirect that energy toward academic success.

The simulated test-taking practice we engage in during BrainMatterZ sessions helps to create just such a mindset change. When students experience that testing environment over and over, complete with my homemade distractions, and they see their scores go up in spite of the distractions, test taking starts to feel easier. Each session, students get excited to beat their last score and overcome the obstacles.

Test simulations are essential for achieving this mindset switch, because while the test-taking environment in the Brain-MatterZ practice sessions are similar to real testing, the stakes are lower. Students can fail, make mistakes, and fail again until they get used to the fact that failure is just another step toward success. With enough test simulation under their belts, students become desensitized to the pressure and cease to see a test environment as an anxiety-provoking situation.

All this comes down to the fact that the more students understand about their own brains and the way neuroplasticity works, the more confident they feel. After all, you can operate any machinery better when you have the manual in hand. In this case, the findings of neuroscience offer today's students a never-before-accessed instruction booklet for the care and maintenance of their own brains.

CHAPTER 9

MYELIN AND CRITICAL PERIODS

The Physiology behind Deep Practice,
Memory, Grit, and How We Form Habits

*I never teach my pupils. I only provide
the conditions in which they can learn.*

ALBERT EINSTEIN

Anyone who has had a child or has been around children knows how incredibly plastic their brains are. Children's brains seem to simply vacuum information from their surroundings—be it the letters of the alphabet, a line from a television show, or that curse word you accidentally let slip. Whatever a child hears, sees, or feels, it sticks in his mind during the developmental period of infancy and childhood, which is known as a critical period for brain development. This phenomenon of superhero-like brain plasticity ends at a certain point, and science has heretofore held the opinion that this phase can never be recovered.

Furthermore, research has shown that whatever children *haven't* heard or seen or felt by the end of the critical period has failed to mold their minds, so if children are not exposed to language, visual stimulus, or touch early on, they are likely to experience immense trouble later on in learning those essential survival skills. But new research shows we can now recreate those critical periods, enabling us to learn new things at rapid rates later in life and to correct the situation of having failed to learn essential things during childhood. This means that learning, both for children and adults, can be made easier than ever before thought.[53] The key to all this is in a discovery called myelin, which grows inside the human brain all the time, but especially during life's critical periods.

CRITICAL PERIODS

Research by Dr. Michael Merzenich, a neuroscientist known today as the father of modern neuroplasticity, shows that the cerebral cortex (the outer layer of the brain) figures out how best to approach any particular problem. Essentially, it constantly teaches itself how to problem-solve based upon the needs of the task at hand. This fact is one of the founding tenets of neuroplasticity: that a certain part of the brain is dedicated to constantly changing and adapting, not just how we do things, but how we learn things.

Because we have this ongoing ability to learn new ways of ingesting information, Merzenich hypothesized that, even as adults, we can still open up the brain, like children, to critical periods, where the mind is far more absorptive than normal. His experiments led him to the conclusion that any learning situation that either requires intense focus or is incredibly interesting or novel will re-initiate this intense period of learning.[54]

Dr. Merzenich's work has been much of the inspiration behind BrainMatterZ. For instance, when I ask a student to stand on the balance board and toss beanbags back and forth while counting down by threes, or when I ask students to build cognitive skills with difficult, timed word searches, I combine the element of focus with the fact that the task is novel. So novel, in fact, are the exercises I invent for the students that I sometimes get funny looks; but the technique works. The more unusual the request, the harder the kids have to concentrate, the more quickly and thoroughly their brains master the cognitive skill.

In BrainMatterZ, I'm not exactly trying to teach students, in that I'm not trying to get them to consciously learn something, like a tutor does. In most cases I'm actually trying to train every student's procedural memory to do things differently without his or her explicit memory having any awareness of the change. When students are forced to focus on a novel task for a certain amount of time, the experience ultimately trains their brains to sustain attention. This is how I open up the student's critical-learning period, train the cerebral cortex in a new way of approaching a problem, and then close the learning period, hopefully with the new habit, or a new set of neuropathways, sealed inside. This approach to brain training is a variation on the deep practice described earlier.

According to Dr. Merzenich, the "plasticity switch" remains on from birth to age ten.[55] These are the years when children absorb the most information and undergo the most brain change. Then, from age eleven onward, the plasticity "off" switch dominates, although it can be triggered under certain conditions. Learning how to trigger that switch back on, so that we can learn and improve ourselves more than ever before, is exactly what Dr. Merzenich's work is about.

Applying the findings of his research is what BrainMatterZ is all about, so let's take a look at these crucial findings. Merzenich's research has shown that the following conditions can trigger the switch:

- Focus or concentration on something
- The surprise of a novel event
- The expectation of either a reward or punishment
- The brain's own positive evaluation of its performance

Through my work as both basketball and cognitive skills coach, I have observed a few other conditions that also seem to create an ideal environment for positive brain change:

- Intensity
- Immediate feedback
- Repetition
- Making the practice harder than the game

With the above criteria in mind, let's look at one example of a learning tool that employed these elements to achieve astounding success: an invention called the "Link Trainer." This device was invented in the 1940s by pilot Edwin Link, Jr.,[56] with the intention of saving lives at a time when airplane crashes during storms were extremely common. The trainer—a working, bathtub-sized model of an airplane's cockpit—enabled pilots to simulate storm conditions, including takeoff, landing, diving, stalling, and recovering, without ever leaving the ground. The dangerous storm conditions were indicated and manipulated by controls and gauges alone, thus condensing the flying experience into just the most difficult scenarios.

This training required immense focus, constantly surprised pilots with novel situations, motivated pilots with the reward of having "crashed" in or "survived" the simulation, and allowed them to immediately know if they had taken the right actions or not. Each and every failure could be followed by a new simulation, a new attempt at success, enabling pilots to reenter the intense training environment as many times as necessary to learn, and enabling them to simulate storm conditions, which were far more arduous than anything they were likely to encounter in real life. The incredible effectiveness of this machine enabled otherwise unremarkable pilots to gain exceptional skill and eventually became responsible for the founding of the United States Air Force in 1947. Today, I think of BrainMatterZ as the high-achieving student's own personal Link Trainer for the mind.

MYELIN

Neurological studies of people undergoing deep practice of various kinds have increased our knowledge of how exactly the brain learns and retains information. The studies have shown that everything we do or think is caused by an electrical signal traveling through a chain of nerve fibers. Just like the electrical wires in your house, these nerve fibers must be insulated in order to channel the message and to increase signal strength. In the brain, a substance called myelin serves as that insulation, wrapping along the length of the nerve fibers.

Unlike the electrical wiring in your house, however, the wiring in your brain can either deteriorate from disuse or improve over time. The more we practice a skill, the more we fire that particular nerve fiber, the more the myelin insulation builds—creating stronger, faster electrical connections around that thought or action.[57] To continue our house metaphor, this would be like if you could, by repeatedly flicking each dim light in your home off and on, actually increase the wattage of the light bulbs until your house glowed like the surface of the sun.

As a coach and ballplayer, I have seen human bodies act like machines. Basketball players wear out their knees, hips, and elbows from frequent use, because they depend upon cartilage, bone, and muscle, which does deteriorate with time; luckily, the brain functions in the exact opposite way. Continuous use of any particular neural pathway makes it stronger in the long run, not weaker. This is why even old weekend-warrior ballplayers like me, who can no longer run as fast or jump as high as they once could, can still remember the plays, techniques, and fundamentals of the game. I progressed from player to coach because even as my body wore out, my mind held onto my accumulated knowledge of the game, due to all those years of repetition and practice. Even now, when I turn on the television to watch a college game or sit in the stands at a high school game, I still feel every move those players make, as well as the ones I feel they should have made, in my bones.

THE IMPORTANCE OF MYELIN
DURING CRITICAL PERIODS

Research into myelin has revealed it tends to build up over time in a series of somewhat unpredictable waves. Anyone who has watched a three-year-old in a ballet class or sports practice has seen this principle at work. While kids this age absorb and repeat every word you say, they often can't remember a simple physical routine from one minute to the next. Different parts of the brain myelinated at different ages and at different rates for different children.[58] But when children do go through myelination waves, such as the early critical period for language, they absorb relevant information with incredible alacrity. Now, neuroscientists are asking, what if adults can also enjoy that incredible level of information absorption? What if, with our ability to improve cognitive skills, we can also open up our brains like children, re-initiating that very same critical period ... at any age?

Studies on rats show that, barring drug intervention, the best way to stimulate a critical learning period is to change the environment inside their cage. When researchers replaced the rats' toys regularly to expose them to new shapes and playthings, the rats' brains showed active engagement in learning, much like when they were babies.[59] This reinforces the idea of novelty being a precursor to opening critical periods in human beings.

As we age, we not only cease to experience natural critical periods, we also tend to settle into routines. Such routines are useful for consolidating learned information but not for reaching out to take in anything new. This is why language immersion courses tend to be so successful in teaching both teens and adults: the novelty of the experience, and its consequent need for total concentration, open the mind up almost like that of a child.

Of course, a life of constant novel experiences is no more useful for learning than one of constant routine. After a certain amount of exposure to a novel experience, that learned information, in order to progress to procedural memory, must become an established part of daily or weekly practice. So a balanced routine of challenging, novel experiences followed by regular practice is really the key to creating and benefitting from new, critical learning periods. This is one of the principles upon which BrainMatterZ is based.

After initially testing a student, I custom design a cognitive skills training program, which combines interest and novelty with an appropriate level of difficulty and repetition. At first students feel very challenged, but over time they improve and become comfortable with the work, up to the point where the knowledge settles into procedural memory. Then, in order to take the student to the next level, I must return him or her to the original phase of novelty and difficulty, or, as we say in athletics, I must "raise the level of play."

AUTOMATICITY

The study of myelin has brought together the discovery of deep practice and that of the explicit and procedural memories. The process of information being transferred from explicit to procedural memory is called "automaticity," and in real life (though not so much in the world of academic testing) this process helps us immensely by freeing up space in the explicit memory for more information to be learned. The more myelin that forms around a particular nerve fiber, the better a student knows the material and the more likely that material is to be transferred out of explicit and into procedural memory. Consequently, testing can be most useful when students are simply required to perform learned skills, instead of explaining how they perform them. Such explanations become harder and harder the better one knows the material, unless the student makes a concerted effort to remember the steps of the activity from the start (which, of course, is twice as much work).

So, writing a grammatically correct essay would be easy for any advanced student, but answering questions about comma usage rules is likely to be much more difficult. Shooting layups could be an easy task for an accomplished basketball player, but teaching a rookie the step-by-step process for this complex skill might be impossible. This is why the old adage, "Those who can, do. Those who can't, teach," is horribly, scientifically incorrect. It should instead read: "Those who can, do. And those who can, also make great teachers, as long as they remember how to break the skill down into a step-by-step process."

Students who tend to be good test takers build myelin around the nerve fibers needed for accomplishing a task as well as around the nerve fibers used in remembering the task's step-by-step process. This is another, more scientific way of explaining why advanced, intermediate, and beginning students should study (and practice sports) together. In many cases, the act of teaching further develops that skill in both teacher and student.

SUBOPTIMAL FIRING

Research into myelin also explains why a student's grit (or resilience or determination) supersedes all other factors in terms of likelihood of collegiate success. In order to create layer upon layer of myelin around the relevant nerve fibers, that circuit must fire "suboptimally."[60] Returning to our house metaphor, that means flicking the switch of a bright lamp in your house will not produce much of an increase in brightness. The light has to be dim to begin with in order for it to benefit from the cycle of repetition. Mistakes must be made, examined, remade, reexamined, and made again, ad infinitum, to enable the learning (and myelin-building) process. We literally, neuroscientifically, build myelin when we make mistakes. So our goof-ups are a big part of our successes!

High-achieving students who get used to learning without mistakes or failure actually learn less than the students who make mistakes more often. When performing tasks they are already good at, students actually reinforce nerve fibers that have already been myelinated, either through early childhood experience, genetic predisposition, or habit. Of course it's a wonderful feeling to be reinforcing while your classmates are all learning, but, in reality, these high-achieving students' classmates are getting smarter and building cognition, while they may not be. If this keeps up, the classmates, growing ever smarter with each challenge they face, will soon surpass the high-achiever. Such students, if they wish to build their intelligence (or if they wish to succeed at a top tier university) must embrace challenges and engage in deep practice at that point, in order to initiate the myelin-building process.

NEURONAL CONNECTIONS

Critical learning periods can be miraculous, but they also can be dangerous. Fascination in something can open the mind up to a critical period, but if that thing turns out to be unhealthy for the person, he or she becomes stuck with a deeply embedded habit that is hard to break. Addictions of all types tend to start with novelty but end with obsession. Drugs, alcohol, smoking, video games, pornography, and even love addictions, because of the highly emotional quality they each generate, can accidentally open up critical learning periods. In these cases, just like when a child learns a language and wants to talk constantly, that new, novel input becomes a source of nearly constant concern. If the person then practices the habit enough to engage automaticity, he or she ceases to be aware that other options exist and that this behavior is a choice. Then the habit becomes much harder to break.

This principle of neuroscience is often described with the following phrase: "Neurons that fire together, wire together." This means that when two stimulants constantly occur together, the brain learns to automatically fire both neurons, even when the person only consciously commanded one of the items to fire. For instance, if for an extended critical period you bandaged two fingers together, the brain would rewire your circuitry so that when you moved one finger, the other would automatically move with it. You would, neurologically speaking, lose the ability to operate these two fingers independently. By the same token, when pleasure is strongly associated with a loved one, it can become difficult for lovers to feel happy apart; when a favorite food is strongly associated with watching television, it can be difficult for the subject to turn on the television without getting hungry; and when relaxation becomes exclusively associated with cigarettes, the mind craves cigarettes whenever it tries to relax. So critical periods—the same neurological factors that help us change our cognition for the better—can also cause unpleasant neurological changes. Of course, opening up critical periods to build cognitive skills is beneficial and has absolutely no negative side effects;

however, the same cannot be said for those who learn bad habits in the same deeply embedded way. What we practice is what we hardwire, so we have to be careful to practice the right things in order to build our brains the way we want.

REVERSING HABITUAL BEHAVIOR

No matter how deeply embedded, bad habits (be they behavioral or cognitive) can almost always be overcome. The key is simply to make a conscious effort to replace them with new, better habits tied to equally strong emotions, using the exact same neurological principle that formed the negative habit to begin with. That is to say, if neurons that fire together, wire together, then neurons that fire apart, wire apart.[61] To break the habit of eating in front of the television, for instance, a subject need only substitute something else enjoyable in the place of the undesired behavior. For instance, why not spend time consciously cultivating the ability to eat at the dinner table and to enjoy pleasant conversation without the presence of the television? Over time, the neurological connection between eating and the television will gradually disappear.

In the same way, students can overcome deficient cognitive skills and their associated habits. For instance, some children, for whatever reason, don't develop the ability to maintain sustained attention, and they grow up with attention deficit problems or just a general sense of being easily distracted. The training in BrainMatterZ is designed to gradually help the student's mind make that neuroscientific connection between attention and studying, until when the "studying" neurons fire, the "attention" neurons naturally accompany it. Just like with the example above, where the subject needed to practice enjoying eating without television, if students want to be able to pay attention for long periods of time, they must practice that skill in order to hardwire it.

SCAFFOLDING

My work in BrainMatterZ also utilizes the principle of "scaffolding," sometimes also called "loading," which stands somewhat in contrast to the technique of using novelty inspired hard work to initiate a critical learning period. With this technique, the student simply builds the myelin sheath, slowly but surely, around relevant neurons, by starting a task at a level where he or she feels comfortable and successful, and by repeating that task, gradually gaining in complexity and difficulty, until the brain's relevant myelin-insulated neurons, which once resembled thin paths, have grown to the size of neuronal superhighways.

For instance, I can use this technique to help a student improve his working memory, a cognitive skill often thought to be the key to intelligence. Working memory is used, for instance, in playing chess. When one has to work out a solution to a problem in one's head, hold it in memory while working out another possible solution to the problem, and then, without moving any of the chess pieces, compare the options and select the best one—that is a great example of working memory in play. Students whose test scores demonstrate low working memory can be scaffolded up to a much higher level by simply practicing these tasks, first at an incredibly simple level, then at incrementally increasing difficulty levels.

EXECUTIVE FUNCTIONS

Myelin doesn't just coat those neurons associated with academics. All neurons require myelin to build skill, and that includes the neurons related to executive functions. These skills govern the personality traits that enable students to persevere and succeed. For instance, the ability to resist temptation and inhibit impulsive action is a skill that must be reinforced for academic success. So is the ability to be cognitively flexible and switch from one task to another without delay. Emotional control is now known to be a learnable skill, too. Organizational skills, self-motivation, and the ability to self-assess are all executive functions and can be learned through repetition at appropriate levels.

Most parents would love their children to be more organized, to be less impulsive, and to have more get-up-and-go, but the fact parents often fail to understand is that these personality traits are also skills and, as such, can be trained. If a student exhibits a lack of skill in one of these executive areas, neuroscientists suggest parents encourage small changes and congratulate the students on each little achievement. A myelin superhighway isn't built in a day, so expecting a student to have an aha moment that leads him or her to sudden overnight change is simply unrealistic and, in most cases, neurologically impossible. Skills like these must be practiced in repetition until they become hardwired into the brain.

The BrainMatterZ program is built to do this very thing. Just like working out at a gym with a personal trainer, students in the program build executive function skills with targeted, professionally designed exercises. And much like anyone who is just getting started working out, having that personal trainer to keep the student on-task and accountable is an invaluable aspect of the program.

Everything we know about myelin reinforces the theory that examined mistakes are the key to growth in any skill or discipline. The sooner students understand that mistakes breed success, the less they will fear test taking, the more they will enjoy learning, and the more likely they will be to take calculated risks and try new things. If we want to enable high-achieving children to be the visionaries of tomorrow, they must understand their own learning processes so that they can enjoy the growth offered to them by cognitive skills training, and then, over the course of a lifetime, continuously increase their intelligence, perseverance, thoughtfulness, organization, self-reflection, and all the other brain functions needed by tomorrow's world-changers and peacemakers.

CHAPTER 10

BRAIN TRAINING ACROSS THE BOARD

Cognitive Skills Training for Everyone

Education is not the learning of facts,
but the training of the mind to think.

ALBERT EINSTEIN

My inspiration for this book has been to inform parents about the latest advances in cognitive skills training so they can help their visionary children succeed with ease, gain self-esteem, and continue to build their brainpower all through life. I have directed this book toward guiding the parents of high achievers, as that is my area of expertise. Naturally, I believe BrainMatterZ is the best program out there specifically for this population, but the parents reading this book probably know students and adults, at a wide variety of levels, who could also benefit from cognitive skills training. With that in mind, in this chapter I am going to provide an overview of some of the major cognitive skills training programs that are out there today, as well as the various types of individuals they specialize in helping. To forestall any future misunderstandings, I will admit to my prejudices right off the bat.

First, there is the computer-training issue. As I have previously stated, research shows all students benefit greatly from learning done in a social setting, which means one-on-one time with a teacher, rather than merely by computer. But, of course, cognitive skills development games are easy and fun to do on the computer, and this method contributes to that sense of efficiency we all love. For this reason, some computer-based companies have gained quite a bit in popularity in the past few years.

The ongoing research these companies conduct seems to show great cognitive advances are being made. However, the training done on the computer is also being tested right there on the computer, which doesn't address the important issue of transference, or whether or not this improvement transfers over into either real life or pencil-and-paper testing environments. Research on transference in this regard is still inconclusive. For this reason—and because computers simply can't provide the ongoing "You can do it!" encouragement of a real, caring person—I recommend against selecting a solely computer-based program, unless that is the only option available to you. I do, however, recommend the use of computer-based training in tandem with programs whose results are known to transfer to real life.

Also, as a licensed educational psychologist, I know how extensive my own education in cognitive skills assessment and training has been and how many courses are required merely to qualify to give the full battery of tests involved in a psychoeducational evaluation (lots!). So, wherever possible, I recommend having every student do his or her cognitive skills development work directly with a licensed professional. The reason is threefold. First, a licensed psychologist knows how to achieve the greatest and most long-lasting cognitive benefit in the shortest amount of time. If my experience is anything to judge from, choosing to go this route can halve the time it takes to achieve your desired results. Second, a licensed psychologist is the only person legally qualified to administer a cognitive assessment, which allows for best-practice results. Finally, long-term student success is highly dependent upon the students having a full understanding of just how very plastic their brains are, since when students understand neuroplasticity is real, they try harder.

At the base level, students must simply understand that neuroplasticity and a growth mindset allow them to take charge of their own brainpower. At a higher level, visionary students will want to gain a full understanding of how and why their brains require repetition, appropriately timed exercises, focus, risk-taking, mistake-making, physical exercise, non-multi-tasking, sensory input, and visual imagery. Science has shown that simply telling students what to do "for their own good" is not as effective as explaining why, scientifically, they must do certain things in certain ways to help their brains develop optimally. A psychologist has the background to explain such things to students in-depth.

Finally, when it comes to taking different types of tests, students need to understand when to engage step-by-step thinking and when to "let it flow," and they need to know why. Psychologists who take the trouble to stay up-to-date on current research can explain these things to students in the course of their cognitive skills training sessions, because, by virtue of their training, they have a keen understanding of such topics. Other teachers and program administrators may or may not stay current on the latest advances in neuropsychology and may or may not understand the importance of imparting it to students.

Another important aspect of any cognitive skills training program is the simple fact that test results have multiple uses. These results are, of course, utilized to establish a baseline for training, but also, when tests show significant discrepancies in cognitive skill levels, these results may qualify students to receive extra time on standardized tests. We discussed earlier why many high achievers need that additional time in order to fully engage all they know to solve a problem, instead of taking shortcuts. More challenged students, obviously, could use that extra time as well. However, in order for test results to ensure a child is legally entitled to extra time, the test must have been administered by a qualified professional. Many of the cognitive skills training programs out there today don't provide qualified test administrators, so, depending upon your needs, this may be something to keep in mind as you select a program for your child, yourself, or any family member or friend.

Parents should ensure that any cognitive skills training program they choose be highly adjustable, child-driven, and, preferably, completely customized for the student. This streamlines the process, enabling students to make exactly the progress they need and to not waste time building skills at which they already excel. This way students benefit from the work level being scaffolded up or down in difficulty as they progress. Work that adjusts with the child's changing skill level in each distinct cognitive area is an important component of any effective program.

Let's begin by discussing two programs designed for students with learning disabilities: Cogmed Working Memory Training and the Arrowsmith Program.

Cogmed, a computer-based program, specializes in cognitive skills training for students with ADHD. It focuses exclusively on improving working memory, which means it does not address the full range of memory, logic, and social/emotional skills that could benefit a child; however, it isn't intended to. Since ADHD is an attention disorder, this program exclusively hones in on the source of that problem.

Cogmed typically operates as a five-week program of five sessions per week, each thirty to forty minutes long. Although the program takes place on a computer, Cogmed does provide a human coach, typically qualified in some education-related area, such as speech and language pathology, educational psychology, or school counseling. And, of course, the coach is trained in the Cogmed system.

These independent coaches, located all over the country, work with Cogmed as part of an established relationship with public and private schools in their areas. The coaches can also be located through the Cogmed website, so, in theory, if you wanted specifically to find an educational psychologist to work as your child's Cogmed coach, and the company has one in your region, you could probably achieve that. The coach conducts an initial interview; monitors daily training; meets with the student once a week, if desired; and provides end-of-session feedback, as well as a six-month, follow-up interview.

The difficulty level of Cogmed's computer-training program constantly adjusts to the user according to a sensitive algorithm. So confident is this company in its algorithm that it tends to de-emphasize any sort of initial testing for the establishment of a baseline. There is no established post-testing program either, so no scientific method exists for calculating the program's benefits. Instead, the company stresses self-assessment. Students make a list of their personal goals and desired outcomes as part of the initial interview and then self-evaluate at the end of the program. Any and all testing, if any, is left entirely up to the child's coach. If the coach happens to be a licensed psychologist, he or she might go ahead and test to establish the child's overall cognitive profile, especially if parents request it, but this is not a part of the Cogmed program.[62]

The Arrowsmith Program, founded by Barbara Arrowsmith-Young, author of the fascinating book *The Woman Who Changed Her Brain*, also operates through qualifying regional schools, but in a very different way. This program aims to help students who have at least average intelligence, but who suffer from any and all learning disabilities. An Arrowsmith classroom is set aside, in participating schools, where a teacher guides qualifying, learning-disabled students through the program for four class periods a day, five days per week, for three to four years. While most learning takes place in this cognitive-skills-centric environment, the program is also structured to enable the students to participate somewhat in the academic world outside the program.

Arrowsmith provides customized programs consisting of computerized, auditory, and pencil-and-paper work. The program's administrators are teachers who also have undergone Arrowsmith's three-week training course. They are not required to have any further qualifications, but they are supervised by an Arrowsmith program coordinator (whose qualifications are not advertised). The teachers enter all student progress into an online database, so parents can view calculated progress reports and other ongoing information. Arrowsmith also monitors its participating schools, offering monthly and year-end assessments of student progress.

Arrowsmith has developed its own Web Assessment—administered via computer with teacher supervision—to establish baselines and test benchmarks for students. To the best of my knowledge, this test is unrelated to any generally-recognized cognitive skills or achievement test. Arrowsmith is, essentially, an intensive program designed for learning-disabled students who want almost complete immersion in daily cognitive skills training in order to emerge three or four years later with (in many cases) the ability to participate in school as a typical student, never setting foot in a special education classroom again.[63]

Next let's look at cognitive skills building programs designed for a general audience. These include BrainHQ and Lumosity.

BrainHQ is geared toward an adult audience of professionals and homemakers who want to remember things better, improve their people skills, and correct problems with things like navigating around town and sustaining attention. A completely computer-based program, BrainHQ is designed for busy people, and, as such, offers two-minute training sessions, which can be done individually or stacked up into hours-long sessions, as desired. The program is described as a "gym for the brain"—a mental supplement to your regular physical workout.

BrainHQ also offers specific courses aimed to help with confident driving, sports skills, hearing in a crowded room, everyday efficiency, alertness, and social fitness, among other topics. It also provides programs specifically for those who have undergone chemotherapy and traumatic brain injury. There is no one-on-one coaching and no baseline testing in this program, but, like the Cogmed program, the computer algorithm adjusts to the needs of the individual.[64]

Lumosity provides a similar service to that of BrainHQ, in that it is computerized, geared for adults, and allows users to choose specific areas where they would like to improve. The initial setup encourages users to select which aspects of each of the executive functions are of most importance to them. For instance, under the heading "Memory," Lumosity offers: remembering patterns; associating names and faces; keeping track of multiple pieces of information; and object/movement sequences. The program offers additional subcategories under the headings "Attention," "Processing Speed," "Flexibility," and "Problem Solving." In that sense, this program is customizable, but since there is no (but the most simplistic) baseline testing, and no post-testing, users are on their own to determine in which areas they would like to work and whether or not they get results. Lumosity is easy to operate and based upon simple games, but it provides no one-on-one training or human oversight.[65] A great deal of self-discipline is necessary in order to develop and maintain brain fitness through a solely computer-based program like this.

As far as cognitive-skills-building courses designed specifically for students, LearningRx is the best known company in the country. Let's take a look at this nationwide franchise, which is designed for the general population of students, alongside my program, BrainMatterZ, which is designed specifically for high achievers.

LearningRx is advertised as a one-on-one cognitive skills building program. Students work at a table, in a game-playing style, with their trainers, in a large room filled with other student/trainer pairs. These trainers are required to have bachelor's degrees and specific LearningRx training. According to LearningRx representatives at the head office, the majority of these trainers are part-time workers, homemakers, retired teachers, and the like.

Programs are advertised as being customized by the trainers for each individual student, but, as with the computerized models, they are actually preset in order to enable the company to keep extensive statistics on their success rates. There are, however, a wide variety of program packages and levels from which to choose. For instance, LearningRx offers separate programs for: seven different cognitive skills; general cognitive skills booster courses for preschool through adult; programs oriented toward skills that help with math; reading comprehension; and many more programs. Within each program, trainers may select bronze, silver, and gold levels, as appropriate for each student.

LearningRx programs typically take place four to five hours weekly, in sixty- to ninety-minute sessions, for periods lasting between twelve and thirty-two weeks, but typically averaging out at eighteen weeks. This means anywhere from forty-eight to one hundred sixty hours of training, the average being eighty-one hours. The sessions take place one-on-one with trainers, although the company also offers a "partner program" where parents work part of that time at home with the students. LearningRx is the only company on this list establishes a baseline with the Woodcock-Johnson cognitive and achievement tests, and then conducts a post-test. These tests, however, are not necessarily administered by qualified personnel, as they are not designed to serve in any capacity except to record student growth statistics for LearningRx and its clients. It is also important to know that no license is required to buy into this franchise, so the centers rely entirely on the LearningRx system and do not necessarily have any psychologist oversight or supervision.[66]

BrainMatterZ, as you know by now, differs from LearningRx and, indeed, from all of the above-listed programs in that it isn't a corporate franchise, nor a program geared at the general population, but that it is a boutique program for high achievers in US (mainly East and West coast), India, and China, to date. We have 1-1 programs, group programs, and summer BrainLabs at Stanford University, UCLA, Pepperdine, and many private schools.. Because I feel I do perform a sought-after and important service, I hope to train more licensed psychologists to do what I do, and to expand, but all in good time. For now, I will sum up BrainMatterZ by saying I offer a one-on-one program as well as a one-on-two program, where up to four students work with myself and an assistant. BrainMatterZ is intended to serve as a supplement to a student's ongoing education, with four components:

- Performance science: Pressure simulations help to desensitize students to performance anxiety.
- Happiness science: I prime students for a happy, grateful, growth-oriented mindset.
- Resiliency science: Grit gets strengthened as students learn about neuroplasticity.
- Brain science: Students participate in customized cognitive skills testing and remediation based upon the conclusions of current brain research.

My extensive, initial battery of tests includes the following areas:

- Cognitive
- Academic
- Processing/memory
- Social/emotional
- Executive functions

With these test results in hand, I hone in on the skills students need to improve upon, while also educating students and parents as to the skills where they already excel. As we work, I adjust the difficulty level of each exercise, as needed, per student.

Often high achievers also suffer from learning deficits of one kind or another. This is one of many areas where BrainMatterZ excels, because the extensive initial testing helps to identify and to remediate those issues right off the bat.

The program typically takes twenty to thirty hours to achieve significant initial results, comparable to those achieved in about four times as many hours in the LearningRx program (according to their published statistics).

I conduct post-testing to show students exactly where they have made gains, and to what degree, and students often return throughout their school careers for boosters, just to keep those skills strong.

COGNITIVE SKILLS PROGRAMS AT A GLANCE

Cognitive skills program	Clients	Format	Typical time period	Licensed psychologist as trainer or overseer	Tests for baseline and progress	Does training transfer?
Cogmed	Students with working memory deficits	Online, computer tasks	12.5 to 18.75 hours	Maybe	Only if requested by parent or suggested by coach	Not consistently
Arrowsmith	Students with learning disabilities and at least average intelligence	In-school, classroom environment, with a teacher	3 to 4 years	No	Arrowsmith provides its own tests	Yes
BrainHQ	General population	Online, computer	Programs in 2-minute increments; no set limit	No	None	Yes
Lumosity	General population	Online, computer	No set limit	No	Lumosity's own "fit test"	Not Consistently
LearningRx	All students and adults	One-on-one	48 to 160 hours	No	Woodcock-Johnson academic and cognitive skills tests	Yes
Brain-MatterZ	Specializes in high-achieving students Students and adults with mild to severe learning disabilities/concussions	One-on-one or small group Both private practice and in-school environments	20 to 40 hours	Yes (required)	Full battery of cognitive, academic, processing, social/emotional, and executive functiontests	Yes
Mediated Learning	All levels of students or adults with learning disabilities	In-school, classroom environment, with a teacher	Yearly curriculum	No	None	Yes

Now that you understand the amazing advances in personal potential that cognitive skills training makes available to all of us, I hope you will pursue some kind of cognitive skills training, not just for your visionary children, but also for yourself and other loved ones. We can all become smarter and happier by improving our brains, and, better yet, we can stave off what many have come to think of as the inevitable mental decline of old age. Yes, brains do produce less myelin with age, and it takes hard work to keep up the sharpness of youth, but the science of neuroplasticity assures us we all have potential to build our brains throughout life.

CHAPTER 11

FROM CHEMOTHERAPY
TO COCHLEAR IMPLANTS

The Future of BrainMatterZ

The best way to predict your future is to create it.

ABRAHAM LINCOLN

Cognitive skills training can, of course, help everyone, not just ambitious students. Research shows that people with all kinds of mental impairments, even severe ones, should be able to benefit from such work. We now know that even when a brain has been damaged, training can help brains find new pathways to old information. Scientists used to believe—and it is still considered common knowledge—that certain areas in the brain correspond to different learning processes, such as language, logic, emotion, and so forth. This isn't considered strictly true anymore, nor is it exactly untrue, it's just that it is too simplistic a view of the brain.

We now know that the brain is far more flexible and adaptable than that. Think of the neurons, axons, and dendrites—the electrical pathways of the brain—as superhighways, state roads, and country lanes, respectively. (This is an incredibly simplistic description of what is obviously a far more complex structure, but, for our purposes, the metaphor holds true.) If, because of disease, brain damage, or disuse, a mental superhighway gets shut down, the mind is actually able to reroute the electrical impulses down a state road, to a country lane, through a back alley, along a deer path, back onto a dirt road, and eventually to its destination. The brain, no matter what age, has that ability to grow and change and adapt to changing conditions, utilizing novel areas to relearn old functions.

I'm not saying it's easy to train a damaged brain to re-navigate like this. It takes hard work, just like it takes hard work for visionary students to improve their cognitive skills. But when your brain isn't functioning properly, nothing is more important for your happiness, security, and self-esteem than getting it back into working order. Luckily, extensive neurological studies have begun to teach us how to achieve this rerouting, and those studies keep on coming up with new ways to help all kinds of people.

Studies on the issue of transference (or the brain's ability to transfer computerized cognitive skills training to real-life situations) are still inconclusive, but studies on one-on-one training have proven cognitive skills training effective, time and time again. As a result, I have been approached by physicians wishing to study the effects of BrainMatterZ training on two interesting populations: cancer survivors suffering from chemotherapy-induced "brain fog," and formerly deaf children trying to adjust to new cochlear implants.

BRAIN FOG

Brain fog—or a reduction in processing speed and the general ability to think, remember, and reason—occurs in some patients as a long-term effect of chemotherapy. Studies have shown this is caused by changes in brain structure similar to what is experienced by a sufferer of brain injury. A Stanford University study suggests cognitive skills training can help these people reroute neurological impulses around the damaged areas.[67] Numerous studies on using computerized brain training are already underway, but in the coming months and years I will be working with researchers to further investigate the long-term effects of one-on-one brain training on this particular population.

The results of our study will better enable neuroscientists to develop a follow-up program for cancer sufferers that truly returns them to full function. I am proud to be able to provide the BrainMatterZ program to help advance the science of neuroplasticity in this way, which I feel is so very important for the future of everyone on this planet. My goal as a brain trainer has always been to help anyone who wishes to improve his or her brain and mind to do so as efficiently and effectively as possible. The way I think of it, eliminating brain fog is basically what I have been doing since the inception of this program. It's just that people experience that fog in different ways, to differing degrees, and for different reasons.

COCHLEAR IMPLANTS

An upcoming cochlear implant study is going to be very interesting, because, with these subjects, the BrainMatterZ training won't be correcting something that has gone wrong in the brain, such as the brain fog study, nor will it be fine-tuning an otherwise well-functioning brain, as I do with students. Instead, BrainMatterZ will be using cognitive skills training to teach the brain a skill it never had before: hearing.

Most people, understandably, believe that we see with our eyes and hear with our ears, but in reality we see and hear with our brains. The eyes and ears provide the initial neurological impulses that make it all happen, of course, but the brain interprets them. When damaged ears fail to provide those impulses, deafness occurs. Cochlear implants provide tiny microphones that bypass the damaged auditory sensors in the ear and that send signals directly to the auditory nerve, which communicates with the brain.[68]

Deaf children typically receive cochlear implants between the ages of two and six, when they are still in the critical period for learning speech and language skills; however, cognitive delays often accompany congenital deafness, resulting in children's brains not interpreting the verbal sounds they hear as speech.[69]

Even with extensive training by speech and language patholo-gists, this inability to recognize speech can persist. Because of the children being in that critical period for language learning, time is of the essence in these situations; so now scientists in the field are also reaching out to psychologists such as myself, looking for new ways to improve the executive functioning skills—including processing speed, working memory, concentration, organization, inhibition, and integration—that are strongly associated with the process of learning speech and language.[70] I am excited to use the BrainMatterZ program in an upcoming cochlear implant study, as part of research into this important field.

The science of neuroplasticity is still quite young, and, as re-searchers learn more about how the brain works and how to help it work better, I plan to stay on the cutting edge. Time will surely reveal many more ways I can use the latest science to help visionary children achieve their world-changing goals. I intend to continue developing BrainMatterZ and informing people about cognitive skills training, until this crucial training becomes a part of every child's education and every parent's childcare routine.

The world we live in really can become a more peaceful, equitable, safe, creative, and healthy place, but it's going to take smart people who can think outside of established structures to achieve it. All children represent the future of this planet, but my focus, because of the teaching and learning background I have had, is on those children who show a propensity early on for be-coming those visionaries who stand out from the crowd.

In my previous careers as basketball coach, academic, and teacher, I saw so many ambitious people fail to achieve their dreams for reasons they simply couldn't understand. Sadly, de-pression and frustration often result from such dashed hopes. My dream is to ensure that when these failures to thrive are due to cognitive skills deficits, that they will never happen again. In fact, I look forward to the day when cognitive skills testing is viewed the same way people view checking their automobile fluids, mon-itoring their blood pressure, or testing the smoke detectors in their homes. After all, we don't leave our health, safety, or auto maintenance to chance, so why should we just assume our brains are functioning optimally?

Because we now know that brains can be tuned up, just like our automobiles, homes, and, to a great extent, our bodies, there is no sense in failing to do so, especially when it comes to helping children become their best. Of course, along with testing comes that all-important brain training process, which can be likened to a regular gym workout, a habit of updating your computer software, or changing the oil in your car to keep it in tiptop condition.

Improving cognitive skills—both when preparing for tests and just to keep in peak form for life's everyday challenges—makes us better, smarter, happier, more successful people. It is my hope that by sharing the information in this book, parents, educators, and researchers might begin to work as a team in order to apply new knowledge and help our young people to "suit up" and become champions in the most significant game of all: life.

END NOTES

1. Sian Beilock, Choke (New York: Free Press, 2010), 9-36.

2. Dr. Michael Merzenich, Soft-Wired (San Francisco: Parnasus Publishing, LLC, 2013), 157-191.

3. Norman Doidge, MD, *The Brain That Changes Itself* (London: Penguin Books, 2007), 45-92.

4. Paul Tough, How Children Succeed (New York: First Mariner Books, 2012), 31-34.

5. Kathleen R. Hopkins, Teaching How to Learn in a What-to-Learn Culture (San Fransciso: Jossey-Bass, 2010).

6. Merzenich, Soft-Wired, 20-24.

7. Ibid.

8. Ibid.

9. Daniel Coyle, The Talent Code (New York: Bantam Books, 2009), 30-35, 38-46.

10. Merzenich, Soft-Wired, 20-24.

11. Coyle, The Talent Code, 51.

12. Ibid.

13. Ibid., 54-73.

14. Ibid.

15. Ibid., 151-162.

16. Anastasia Tryphon and Jacque Vonèche, eds. Piaget Vygotsky: The Social Genesis of Thought (New York: Psychology Press, 1996).

17. Shawn Achor, The Happiness Advantage (New York: Virgin Books, 2011), 39, 50.

18. Ibid., 58.

19. Ibid., 44.

20. Ibid., 53.

21. Marcial Losada, "Work Teams and the Losada Line: New Results," Positive Psychology News Daily, December 9, 2008, http://positivepsychologynews.com/news/guist-author/200812091298

22. Marcial Losada "The Complex Dynamics of High Performance Teams," Mathematical and Computer Modeling 30 (1999):179-192; Marcial Losada and Emily Heaphy, "The Role of Positivity and Connectivity in the Performance of Business Teams: A Nonlinear Dynamics Model," American Behavioral Scientist 47(6) (2004): 740-765; Barbara L. Frederickson and Marcial F. Losada, "Positive Affect and the Complex Dynamics of Human Flourishing," American Psychologist 60(7) (2005): 678-686.

23. Robert H. Frank, Luxury Fever (Princeton, New Jersey: Princeton University Press, 2010).

24. Brendan Wilde, "Study Shows Meditation Changes Brain Structure in Just Eight Weeks," Family Health Guide, accessed June 9, 2014, http://www.familyhealthguide.co.uk/mindfulness-meditation-leads-to-increases-in-brain-gray-matter-density-in-just-8-weeks.html

25. Paul Tough, How Children Succeed (New York: Houghton Mifflin Harcourt Publishing, 2013), 72.

26. Ibid., 74-5.

27. Ibid., 76.

28. Ibid., 72.

29. Ibid., 73.

30. Carol S. Dweck, "The Perils and Promises of Praise," Educational Leadership 65(2) (October 2007): 34-39.

31. John Medina, Brain Rules (Seattle: Pear Press, 2008), 172.

32. Marina Krakovski, Stanford Alumni Magazine (March-April 2007), http://alumni.stanford.edu/get/page/magazine/article/?article_id=32124

33. Medina, Brain Rules, 16.

34. Ibid., 10-14.

35. Ibid., 14-15.

36. Ibid., 18.

37. Ibid.

38. Ibid., 75-80.

39. Ibid., 85.

40. Ibid., 89.

41. Ibid., 199-219.

42. Ibid., 173.

43. Ibid., 176-178.

44. David Hyerle, A Field Guide to Using Visual Tools (Alexandria, VA: Association for Supervision and Curriculum Development [ASCD], 2000).

45. Medina, Brain Rules, 233-236.

46. Beilock, Choke, 36.

47. Ibid., 34.

48. Ibid., 35.

49. Ibid., 88.

50. Ibid., 34.

51. Ibid., 43.

52. Ibid., 139.

53. Doidge, The Brain That Changes Itself, 45-92.

54. Doidge, The Brain That Changes Itself, 83.

55. Merzenich, Soft-Wired, 38-45.

56. Coyle, *The* Talent Code, 20-24.

57. Coyle, *The* Talent Code, 32.

58. Coyle, *The* Talent Code, 45.

59. Takao K. Hensch Ph.D. and Parizad M. Bilimoria Ph.D., "Reopening Windows: Reopening Critical Periods for Brain Development," The Dana Foundation (August 29, 2012): 3, accessed June 13, 2014, https://dana.org/Cerebrum/2012/ Re-opening_Windows__Manipulating_Critical_Periods_for_ Brain_Development/

60. Coyle, *The* Talent Code, 43.

61. Doidge, *The* Brain That Changes Itself, 62-66.

62. http://www.cogmed.com/

63. http://www.arrowsmithschool.org/

64. http://www.brainhq.com/why-brainhq/about-the-brainhq-exercises

65. http://www.lumosity.com/

66. http://www.learningrx.com/

67. Susan Young Rojan, "Brain Training May Help Clear Cognitive Fog Caused by Chemotherapy," MIT Technology Review (May 17, 2013), http://www.technologyreview.com/news/514876/brain-training-may-help-clear-cognitive-fog-caused-by-chemotherapy/

68. National Institute on Deafness and Other Communication Disorders. "Cochlear Implants." Last modified November 2013. https://www.nidcd.nih.gov/health/hearing/pages/coch.aspx

69. John S. Oghalai M.D., "Optical Neuro-Imaging of Deaf Children with Cognitive Delays after Cochlear Implantation," The Dana Foundations, http://www.dana.org/Media/GrantsDetails.aspx?id=39045

70. "Indiana University, Speech Research Laboratory. Neurocognitive Processes in Deaf Children with Cochlear Implants (RO1DC009581)." http://www.iu.edu/~srlweb/research/neurocognitive-processes-in-deaf-children-with-cochlear-implants-ro1-dc009581/

Made in the USA
San Bernardino, CA
14 April 2019